SPIRITUAL
HEALING

SPIRITUAL HEALING

An Objective Study
of a Perennial Grace

by

D. CARADOG JONES

Foreword by

**THE REV. CANON
C. E. RAVEN, D.D., F.B.A.**

and a Doctor's Comment by

J. BURNETT RAE, M.B., Ch.B.
*Vice-Chairman of the
Churches' Council of Healing*

1724

LONGMANS, GREEN AND CO
LONDON . NEW YORK . TORONTO

LONGMANS, GREEN AND CO LTD
6 & 7 CLIFFORD STREET LONDON WI
BOSTON HOUSE STRAND STREET CAPE TOWN
531 LITTLE COLLINS STREET MELBOURNE

LONGMANS, GREEN AND CO INC
55 FIFTH AVENUE NEW YORK 3

LONGMANS, GREEN AND CO
20 CRANFIELD ROAD TORONTO 16

ORIENT LONGMANS LTD
CALCUTTA BOMBAY MADRAS
DELHI VIJAYAWADA DACCA

First Published 1955

Printed in Great Britain by
ADLARD & SON LIMITED
BARTHOLOMEW PRESS, DORKING

The man who holds miracles to be ceased puts it out of his own power ever to witness one.

BLAKE

What is very startling . . . is the abundance of testimony given by those who have had intimate experience of man's spiritual life to the conviction that in the early stages prayer receives literal fulfilment with great frequency; that later on this becomes less frequent, until it seems almost to cease, as though God at first gives encouragement of the most obvious kind and later withdraws this in order to evoke a deeper trust.

The proper outline of a Christian prayer is not 'Please do for me what I want'. It is 'Please do with me what You want'. That prayer will always be answered in proportion to its sincerity.

WILLIAM TEMPLE

FOREWORD

By the Rev. Canon C. E. RAVEN, D.D., F.B.A.

*Late Regius Professor of Divinity in the
University of Cambridge*

THE purpose of a Foreword is conventionally two-fold — to assure the reader that the volume thus prefixed 'supplies a long felt want' and that the author is qualified for the task that he has undertaken. There have not been many recent books for which such a guarantee can be more confidently given.

One of the most remarkable features of recent Christian activity has been the revival of the ministry of healing, not only among the disciples of Mrs Eddy but in all denominations. Pilgrimages to Lourdes, services for the laying on of hands, centres of spiritual healing, and lectures and literature on the subject all testify to the claim that physical health is now, as in the New Testament, recognized as among the good gifts which Christ gave to men. Psychology and psychiatry have made a large if mainly indirect contribution to this revival; and the sufferings arising out of two world wars have been its occasion and opportunity. Very many people not otherwise attracted by religion have had their interest aroused by records of cures, miraculous or at least outside ordinary medical and surgical practice. And though there has been much criticism and in some cases much disappointment, the conviction that there are resources available to faith and operating through prayer has become widespread if not yet universal among Christians.

Yet in fact for most of us the problems which such a claim inevitably raises have remained unanswered. Most of us would agree that if a firm belief in the efficacy of the healer can be aroused remarkable results will follow. But whether such faith is the sole essential condition, or whether the techniques used by various healers are important, or whether there is a radical difference in scope and efficacy between the Christian exorcist and the Zulu witch-doctor, between the healings at Lourdes and the cures of M. Coué at Nancy — such questions remain, for many of us at least, unanswered. And, so far as I am aware, no one has hitherto set himself to collect and describe the cases in which the material for an answer can be found.

At such a time when widespread and often strongly emotional interest has been aroused, and when there is urgent need for the exercise of a wise judgment, the evidence which Mr Caradog Jones has so carefully gathered and so accurately stated is of the highest importance.

The book does not profess to answer the sort of questions which the sceptical enquirer will raise. It does not undertake the analysis and interpretation of the material. To do so would involve a profound research into fundamental problems of theology and philosophy, of psychology and physiology; and a generation which has abandoned its reliance upon quantitative methods and mechanistic analogies, and has in consequence rediscovered its awareness of the limitations of our human intelligence and its conviction that man's reach exceeds his grasp without having yet found satisfactory explanations of psychic phenomena, of extra-sensory perception or even of telepathy,

viii

must be content to wait for fuller knowledge before proceeding to dogmatic assertions. But the case-histories here presented will convince any unprejudiced reader of the importance of the whole subject and will go far towards equipping him with the sort of evidence on which he can form a reasonable judgment. It is not for me to express a verdict: but it is hardly disputable that Mr Caradog Jones has established a very strong case for the efficacy of intercessory prayer; that he has shown that its effects are not limited to cases of nervous or mental disease; and that the results achieved cannot be fully explained in terms of the faith of the patient or the willpower of his friends or even the personality of the healer. Old-fashioned physicians used to speak of the *Vis medicatrix Naturae*: we in face of the evidence before us can anglicize this sentiment and speak of the healing power of God.

Mr Caradog Jones has been at pains to obtain and verify his material objectively and critically. He sets out the details of the steps that he has taken to safeguard his readers from emotional and untested claims or from records of temporary and casual betterment. Even so, as he warns us, he has understated the cases and done his best to allow for the tendency to dramatize and exaggerate. Too often such records (which may well be genuine) have been presented to us in a form which proclaims not only a strongly suggestible and imaginative temper in the recorder, but an obvious readiness to evade difficulties and to resent criticism. It is important that a subject like this should be handled by one who has been trained in the objective and impartial presentation of evidence, who knows the difficulties of social investigation, and who combines knowledge of his subject with sound judgment and the ability to discount not only the prejudices of his witnesses but his own bias towards wishful thinking.

Of his capabilities for such a task our author's record of previous work is sufficient proof. It was my privilege to meet him when he was on the staff of Liverpool University and engaged upon the Social Survey of Merseyside. His skill in devising methods of investigation was as remarkable as his insight into the points of special importance when planning his work and his wisdom and objectivity in estimating its results. His friendship meant much to me then and means much to me now. He seems to have precisely the qualities necessary for research of this kind; and now that he has gathered, arranged and presented his evidence I hope that he will be encouraged to carry forward the investigations and interpretations for which the present study is an indispensable preparation.

PREFACE

A work of this nature could not have been compiled without the willing co-operation of many people. I think especially of those who introduced me to patients, of some who went to considerable trouble in helping me to get the detailed particulars I wanted, and of the patients themselves who were most considerate in their readiness to answer the many questions I put to them. Having undertaken to treat their information as confidential, I cannot thank them by name, but I feel sure they will know how greatly I appreciated their help.

Dr C.P.Blacker, a distinguished psychiatrist, Consultant to the Bethlem Royal Hospital and the Maudsley Hospital, and Sir Russell Brain, President of the Royal College of Physicians, were good enough to read my script. Both made valuable comments which have influenced my thought on the subject; but of course I take sole responsibility for the way in which it is presented here.

I have had, too, throughout the help and advice of my brother, Dr T. Henry Jones, formerly County Medical Officer of Surrey, and the constant encouragement of my wife, who has read the proofs with me.

In conclusion I must thank Canon Raven for his stimulating and generous Foreword, and Dr Burnett Rae for so very kindly offering, when he had seen my script, to add 'A Doctor's Comment'. This certainly merits close attention, for it is the considered conclusion of a specialist in psychiatry who has given much thought to the subject of spiritual healing over a period of forty years following both a medical and a theological training.

D. CARADOG JONES

CONTENTS

CONTENTS

CONTENTS

PART III

INDIAN RECORDS

PART IV

A DOCTOR'S COMMENT
by J. Burnett Rae, M.B., Ch.B.

Part One

INTRODUCTION

Origin of the Work

In 1951 the Eugenics Society arranged for a reprint of a book written by its founder, Sir Francis Galton, and originally published just over seventy years ago. Galton was a Fellow of the Royal Society, a cousin of Charles Darwin, and himself a man of eminently fertile mind. The book in question broke new ground in its day. Its title was *Inquiries into Human Faculty*, and the first edition contained three chapters which were omitted from subsequent editions. In one of these chapters the objective efficacy of prayer was discussed and the author came to the conclusion, on the statistical evidence he submitted, that prayer had no objective efficacy. In view of this it may surprise those who know little about Galton that he was a man imbued with a strong religious sense, who treated the opinions of those who differed from him with more respect than they sometimes accorded to his. He had no doubt whatever that prayer could be of help to the person who prayed, but the broad result of his analysis was that one person, by prayer alone, could not help another person or exert any influence upon future events. This, if true, would undermine a fundamental Christian belief.

Under the impression that a great many people today have reached the same conclusion, not because they have attempted seriously to examine the evidence, as Galton did, but because in their own experience they fail to see anything very definite happen as the result of prayer, I thought it worth while to collect fresh evidence on the subject. I do not propose to discuss Galton's work, for I came early to the decision that a general statistical treatment of the question, such as he attempted, was not suited to the purpose in view. There are too many complicating factors involved.

In the present work prayer is taken to be, not merely petitioning, but communion with God in a more intimate sense. The question at issue is whether such communion brings into action spiritual forces capable of influencing not only the person who engages in prayer but others also on whose behalf prayer is offered. We have a test of such a possibility when a friend or relation prays for the recovery of one who is ill, especially when the illness is so severe that the doctors consider the case hopeless; for it is claimed that prayer offered in such circumstances, either with or without the patient's knowledge, sometimes results in a changed outlook on life on the part of the patient, and that this may be accompanied by a complete cure of his ill condition.

Spiritual Healing

This is a type of what is termed spiritual healing and I have heard in the course of my inquiries of a surprisingly large number of prayer groups scattered throughout the country that endeavour to help sick people in this way. There are also, as is well known, several organisations[1] whose function it is to encourage the formation of such groups and to promote the

[1] Particulars about some of these organisations will be found in Appendix One.

practice of spiritual healing. Some are connected with the Church of England, or another branch of the Christian Church; others are interdenominational in character. The possibility of such healing is regarded by them as a fundamental doctrine, and its practice is general with such a body as the Christian Scientists.

I shall refer here to one organisation only, in order to draw attention to the degree to which the more enlightened clergy and doctors now work together in this field. In 1944 Archbishop Temple set up a committee to go into the question of spiritual healing and the outcome was the formation of 'The Churches' Council of Healing'. One aim of the Council is 'to afford a recognized basis for the co-operation of doctors and clergy in the study and performance of their respective functions in the work of healing, and to promote this co-operation in thought and action throughout the country'. The President of this body is Dr. Fisher, the present Archbishop of Canterbury, and the British Medical Association is officially represented on it, as also are most of the Christian Churches except the Roman Catholic.

In a supplement to the *British Medical Journal* (8 November 1947), under the heading 'Medicine and the Church', a statement appears concerning the relationship between The Churches' Council of Healing and the British Medical Association. This was approved by the Council of the B.M.A. and I quote an extract from it:

It would seem desirable that the whole field of medical practice in relation to the work of the Church should be explored. Moral aspects in the cause, treatment and prevention of disease cannot be overlooked. . . . Medicine and the Church working together should encourage a dynamic philosophy of health. . . . Health is more than a physical problem, and the patient's attitude both to illness and to other problems is an important factor in his recovery and adjustment to life. Negative forces such as fear, resentment, jealousy, indulgence and carelessness play no small part in the level of both personal and national health.

These remarks apply with particular force to any form of mental illness. There is a growing conviction among medical men that the patient's outlook on life may not infrequently be largely responsible for the physical symptoms from which he suffers: hence the importance of continuous psychiatric research into these causal factors, as conducted, for instance, at the Maudsley Hospital in London, and the value of the kind of approach to mental illness that is fostered in such institutions as the Rehabilitation Centre at Roffey Park in Sussex and The Retreat at York. It may not be unfitting to recall here that The Retreat, started by members of the Religious Society of Friends in 1796, has the distinction of being the first hospital in England where mental patients received the kindly Christian treatment which has long since become general practice. In view of the readiness on the part of high authorities in Church and Medicine to collaborate in the cure of the sick, to which attention has been directed above, it is clear that spiritual healing cannot be regarded as the concern only of quacks and charlatans: the question of its validity is one that deserves serious examination.

There is an evident revival of interest in spiritual healing in our generation, to which the setting up of a new Commission of Inquiry by the present Archbishop of Canterbury bears testimony. Students of the subject will be well aware that throughout history, with time gaps, accounts of such cures have been recorded in different countries. These cures are frequently associated with shrines and holy places and are attributed to the Virgin Mary or to a saint of the Roman Catholic Church. Lourdes is one of the most famous places of pilgrimage and it has become the centre of an International Medical Association. Alleged cures are very carefully sifted and examined by several doctors before they are officially accepted and approved.[2] Readers of the Journals of George Fox and John Wesley will recall instances of remarkable cures in our own country.

Coming nearer to our own time, one of the most noted healers in the first half of the present century, James Moore Hickson, conducted a five years' Christian Healing Mission round the world, ending in April 1924. He visited the United States, Canada, India, China, Japan, the Philippines, Egypt, Palestine, Paris, Rome, Africa, Australia and New Zealand. No one reading the account of this tour in his *Heal the Sick* (Methuen, 1924) can fail to be impressed by the audiences he drew, the enthusiasm of his reception everywhere he went, and the laudatory terms in which clergy occupying high office and other responsible people referred to his mission. It is worthy of note that the physical healings, remarkable as the records are, were judged, no doubt rightly, to be of less concern than the spiritual effects of Hickson's ministry.

Data for the Present Inquiry

The records I have collected relate to people who have been healed of some physical or mental disability

[2] See Appendix Two for a Note on the Cures at Lourdes.

or illness, and in general it is their belief that the healing has come in response to prayer, often — though not always — accompanied by the laying on of hands by someone to whom the gift of healing is attributed. Such evidence concerning prayer is as good an approach to the objective in character as one could get. As it was necessary for my purpose to get first-hand data, I have confined myself to present-day records. Also my cases come in the main from Britain, although a few from the United States and India have been included in order to discover how far they all have features in common. The Indian cases are assembled together in Part III for the reasons there given. The tabular analysis of some of these cases, supplied by Bishop Q, is worthy of special attention in view of his long experience as a healer and the systematic way in which he kept his records (see p. 111). Whether the cures described in this book occurred in America or Britain, in the East or the West, a close parallel will be noted in the procedure adopted in most of them.

I have obtained all my facts from the person healed or from someone very closely concerned with the case. I have heard about them in the first instance through friends, sometimes medical friends, or through references in books or daily papers. In my first approach I have explained quite frankly the purpose of the inquiry and I have undertaken not to make any names public, so as to avoid arousing idle curiosity which might be unwelcome. Fictitious names or initials are therefore used throughout, but I retain in my files all the letters and other data which make up the raw material of the book. The only exceptions to the anonymity rule occur in the very few cases where some record of them has already appeared in print to which I have had access. The material has had to be sifted, checked and edited to enable me to present the facts of each case in the manner best suited to my purpose. But I have not departed materially from what has been told to me. If anything, my tendency has been to 'write down' rather than to 'write up' each case, using as far as possible the actual words of my correspondents though usually omitting quotation marks. Words are an expression of the personalities of those using them and they should consequently help the reader to form his own judgment as to the value of their evidence.

This much I can say: I am satisfied that all the people whose stories I have recorded were perfectly honest in their belief that their healing could be attributed, in whole or in part, to the power of the Divine Spirit taking possession of them either directly or through the ministration of others, in response to prayer or communion with this Spirit. It is possible, of course, to believe them to be honest and yet to doubt the evidence of their senses. To those who take that view I call to mind a singularly apt comment made by a lady, quite justifiably, at the end of a letter to me after she had very patiently answered a number of rather searching questions I had put to her: 'I feel like the blind man whom Jesus had healed, and they kept questioning him about it afterwards until at last he said "All I know is that once I was blind and now I can see". My answer to you is, "Once I was in agony in neck, head and ears, and now I am not." ' That ninth chapter of St. John's Gospel, from which she quoted, has always struck me as being true to life; the behaviour of everyone in the story is so perfectly natural.

If we are prepared to accept the evidence of these witnesses that they have been healed, an attempt must be made to determine what weight is to be given to medical treatment in their recovery. The opinion of the patient, however certain he may be in his own mind, is not always to be trusted on this point, and the questions asked about each case were designed to throw additional light on it. If the patient had not been seen by a doctor for some time, as happened in several of my cases, there was less likelihood that medical treatment was the main healing influence, although we cannot exclude the possibility that it was necessary.

Those who practise psycho-therapy will claim that suggestion may have played a large part in many of the cures recorded. That undoubtedly is true, but we must be careful here of our terminology: what some people call suggestion, others call faith. Recalling one sentence in the paragraph already quoted from the *British Medical Journal*: 'the patient's attitude both to illness and to other problems is an important factor in his recovery,' the aim of both psycho-therapist and spiritual healer is to develop the right attitude in the patient. The former perhaps suggests to him that he can get perfectly well if he will only make use of his resources and pull himself together; the latter says that the healing power of God is available to those who put their faith in Him, and possibly prayer is offered that the patient may turn to God in his need, prepared to accept whatever He sends. Is there any radical contradiction between these two approaches? Both may be needed; the effort that the patient makes to get better by every available means may sometimes be an essential preparation for spiritual healing. Moreover, neither psycho-therapist nor healer will venture to claim that the healing power resides in himself: he is only the mediator. Any special ability each may have for drawing out the best in a patient to the benefit of mind and body is a talent to be cultivated and used, just like the skill and experience of the family doctor.

Whichever terms the reader pleases to use, some persons are known to be much more 'suggestible' or to have more 'faith' than others, and they are more likely to be cured because they themselves co-operate with the physician or healer. It is not unreasonable to believe that usually we contribute in some measure to our own healing, so answering in part our own prayers. But while such co-operation may be noted in nearly all the cases which I record, it certainly cannot be claimed that a strong expectation of healing was always present; and when absent the power of suggestion, in the more limited sense of the term, could not be very effective. In fact, a few cases are included in my series where the patient was too young to understand what was happening; dependence had to be on the faith and prayers of others: direct suggestion was ruled out.

If some cures occur with little or no faith on the part of the patient, it might be expected that one with much faith will certainly be cured. The truth, however, is that, even given a large measure of faith on the part of the patient, healing is by no means assured. This is puzzling and a source of discouragement to many, for it must be admitted that the impression gained by a close study of the subject is that the proportion of persons permanently cured by spiritual healing is not high. We have here what may seem at first sight a state of affairs difficult to reconcile with our conception

9

of the nature of the Divine Will, and the dilemma can only be resolved if we acknowledge that our vision is limited to the present time and the present world. We have to rest satisfied with the reflection that in all probability healing is withheld when, to the far-seeing eye of the Creator of the Universe, that will best contribute to the growth in grace of the patient or of those within his sphere of influence.

Analysis of Information Obtained

The particulars I tried to get concerning each of my cases were as follows:

1. Sex and age of patient.
2. Precise description of disease, disability or illness from which the patient suffered.
3. How long had suffering lasted?
4. Clear account of the steps taken which led to recovery.
5. Was recovery immediate or gradual? If gradual, how long did it take?
6. How long has it lasted? Give dates if possible.
7. Was the patient undergoing any medical treatment at the time of cure, to which it might conceivably have contributed? If so, what was the nature of the treatment?
8. Was the cure complete or has there been any recurrence of the trouble? If a recurrence, when and how severe was it?
9. What was the reaction of the doctor on first seeing the patient after recovery?

Also, I usually added a note that it would be helpful if the names and addresses of the patient, the doctor, and the minister through whom the cure was effected could be given, for reference only, not for publication.

These questions are for the most part self-explanatory. The age of the patient is a factor affecting the likelihood of an easy recovery. It is important to know whether the trouble has been long-standing. If healing is only gradual, more credit may have to be given to medical treatment than the patient realizes, and to the fact that rest is in itself often a great aid to recovery. Hence the importance of question seven. In the excitement of a novel situation, perhaps in public and with the laying on of hands, the patient may experience relief from pain at the time but it may return later. On the other hand, what appears to be a complete recovery may take place and last for some time, with or without a recurrence of the same or similar symptoms eventually. The answer to question nine is often illuminating.

There is a wide variety of cases among my records which, acting on medical advice, I have classified under four heads: Conditions Associated with the Nervous System, Inflammatory Conditions, a Casualty Section, and Constitutional Abnormalities. I start with those, such as certain forms of mental derangement, which are a passing condition afflicting a person for a season only; between attacks he seems to be quite normal. Such symptoms might be expected to yield to spiritual treatment more readily perhaps than an illness which is physical rather than mental, though it must be admitted that the border line between physical and mental is not precise. There are also physical conditions, such as migraine, which may be due to mental strain. These too might conceivably yield to spiritual treatment and are included early in my list. At the other extreme are bone fractures and similar disabilities which, one would suppose, are much less subject to the control of the mind. I therefore deal with them later. Malignant growths, subnormality and congenital conditions generally, in my arrangement, also come towards the end of the list. Without pretending to be at all exact in my classification, the aim, it will be seen, is to deal first with cases which might more readily respond to a prayerful approach and to come later to those less likely to make such response. Where cases could have been placed under either of two headings, I have chosen that which seemed the more important. Cases 9 and 10, for example, might equally well have been placed under Inflammatory Conditions, but there is no doubt that an attack of asthma is liable to be brought on when the subject is in a frightened or nervous state. It has been suggested to me too that Cases 48 and 49 mght be classed under Nervous System; I have placed them in my last group because the children concerned were subnormal if not abnormal.

One thing I would particularly stress: we must not assume that the explanation given by the patient as to the cause or cure of his illness is always to be trusted, however convinced he may be about it; he may mistake what the doctor has said to him. Nor can we be certain that the diagnosis of the doctor is always infallible. The headings of my cases are as stated by the doctor or patient, and normally one would not expect to get further confirmation. Take, for example, Case 6. The surgeon concerned in this case was said to be the chief brain specialist in the hospitals of a large municipality and his diagnosis was brain tumour. If he was mistaken, and the cause of the woman's condition was a clot on the brain, a high medical authority has pointed out to me that the course of her subsequent recovery would not be unexpected from the medical point of view. Again, it is well known that Mongolian defectives will sometimes show a striking response to treatment that is graced by lovingkindness and patience. That, no doubt, accounts in a measure for the results recorded in Case 49, for in such cases the right approach to the patient makes a world of difference. It might well be claimed that a consistently right approach, in what must often be very difficult and trying circumstances for those who minister to mental patients of any kind, can only be maintained by those who — making no outward profession — themselves seek that silent but continual communion with God which is the essence of prayer.

With the same effort I could, no doubt, have obtained particulars of an equal number of sick people for whom earnest prayers were offered and who were not healed. But my object has been only to discover whether *sometimes* there is an association between a spiritual approach to a patient and his physical and mental betterment, not to prove that such an association is *invariable*. Moreover, it is not out of place to point out that no doctor would claim that all his patients respond to medical treatment. But it would be foolish on that account to imagine that we can get along well enough without doctors. The reader must be left to decide how far the cumulative evidence of healing presented in these pages tells in favour of a spiritual approach in most cases of illness, not in place of but as complementary to the practical skill and knowledge of the physician or surgeon.

The late Dr Alexis Carrel, F.R.S., eminent physiologist and Nobel Prize winner, in his *Man, the Unknown*,[3] expressed the opinion that miraculous cures, 'characterized by an extreme acceleration of the process of organic repair,' seldom occur; and that would appear to be true. He went on to say that 'The only condition indispensable to the occurrence of the phenomenon is prayer. But there is no need for the patient himself to pray, or even to have any religious faith. It is sufficient that someone around him be in a state of prayer. Such facts are of profound significance. They show the reality of certain relations, of still unknown nature, between psychological and organic processes. They prove the objective importance of the spiritual activities. . . . They open to man a new world.'

Whereas I set out to find what evidence there was for the objective efficacy of prayer, my inquiry has turned out to be a case study of spiritual healing. Defining prayer as communion of spirit with Spirit, of man with God, perhaps that is not so far amiss since most healing of the kind here recorded seems to take place when the aim of healer and healed is to establish such communion.

[3] Published originally by Hamish Hamilton in 1935, it was repeatedly reprinted and was translated into several languages.

Part Two

PHYSICAL AND MENTAL
HEALING RECORDS

CONDITIONS ASSOCIATED WITH
THE NERVOUS SYSTEM

1 *Mental Disability*

I first heard of this case from the London vicar who was concerned in it. A young student, taking a degree course in music, was suffering from mental disability. Its effect on her was such that she was quite unable to come to decisions, even about small things at home, and she could not face her music examination. She had treatment for about three months in a mental hospital but with little improvement in her condition. On coming out of hospital she went to stay with friends and later, after her mother's death, she returned home to keep house for her father and brother. During this time she consulted a psychiatrist, but she felt that she was 'getting nowhere, just going round in circles', as she put it to me when I interviewed her.

In the meanwhile, a friend who was interested in spiritual healing persuaded her, much against her inclination for she had no belief in it, to go to hear an address on the subject in a church. The vicar spoke of wholeness or holiness of life and this came to her as a challenge.

For several months she was unwilling to face the challenge, but she came to a point where she 'felt she must accept Christ and His help'. This she did really on the strength of the faith and prayers of people attending the church, who took a personal interest in her and helped her greatly. She confessed that she herself was able only to pray 'Will you help me, though I don't believe?' But it so far worked that she felt a great sense of relief, and she seemed to gain power to overcome the difficulties she had hitherto experienced. It would not be right to say that she never afterwards felt depressed: she did occasionally, but 'not any more than other people'.

She gave up music as a profession, but she finds it of great help in the church work which she has taken up as a career. This church post she has now held for five years and is very happy in it. Incidentally, the psychiatrist who had been treating her was very pleased to hear of her new outlook upon life. Her friend went with her to see him after she had reached the decision which brought about the significant change in her life. To their surprise he showed his appreciation of the step she had taken by going on his knees and praying with them himself.

2   Maniacal Condition

Particulars of this case came from a young doctor with a scientific interest in healing of all kinds. He has a private practice and is attached to a well-known hospital. One of his patients, first seen by him in 1949, was a physically diminutive ex-Salvation Army man slightly over 50 years of age. He had given up God and the Army some four or five years before, because a son-in-law in the R.A.F., for whose safety he had prayed, was shot down towards the end of the war. When Dr. A saw him he was 'raving and maniacal, cursing and swearing, and chucking boots about as if possessed by a demon'. He remained in that condition for nearly a week and the doctor thought he would be obliged to certify him and send him to a mental hospital. His wife was neurotic: that added to his troubles.

Several friends of Dr A were told of the man's condition and were remembering him in their private prayers. The turning point seems to have come after a talk he had with the doctor; he had been very low-spirited, feeling that he had sinned and was beyond repentance and Dr A assured him that he was not. Within twenty-four hours a dramatic change occurred, as if the demon had gone out of him. Since that day, four years ago, according to the latest report I received in November 1953, he has not once raved or been maniacal. In fact both he and his wife had been persuaded to join the church which Dr A himself attended and they had been helping with the Sunday School teaching.

3 *Insanity*

Fred was a casualty of the First World War. At the age of twenty he had gone into it with high ideals, little guessing the horrors that awaited him, and as a result of his experiences he lost his reason. This was his condition twenty years later. He was harmless but had been pronounced hopelessly insane. For ten years he had refused to leave his room and for a year, in spite of all entreaties, he had remained in bed. The story of his remarkable recovery has been published[1] and is briefly summarized here. My attention was drawn to it by

[1] *A Man's Reach*, p. 226, by Glenn Clark (Harper Brothers, New York, 1949); and *Recovery*, pp. 43–46, by Starr Daily (Arthur James, Evesham, Worcs., and Macalester Park Publishing Co., St. Paul, Minnesota).

Dr Glenn Clark, an American professor of literature who is a strong believer in the power of prayer. He told me it was one of the clearest answers to prayer in his experience.

Dr Clark had been visiting Fred over a period of two years but he felt he was making no impression on him. He then wrote to another spiritually minded friend of his, Pastor Roland Brown, and asked him, if ever he was near, to come and see Fred. The result was that together, some time later, they visited him.

Pastor Brown sat silent while Dr Clark entered into conversation with Fred. As Pastor Brown meditated on Fred's plight and the sorrow of his ageing parents, he felt a surge of compassion well up within him and he began to pray silently that God would lift the veil from Fred's mind, banishing the evil spirits of delusion and fear to which he appeared to be subject. At this point Dr Clark suddenly asked Fred what was his idea of the demons which Jesus had cast out. To his surprise this answer came pat: 'To be possessed by a demon is to be obsessed with a half-truth; for instance, if a lion were caught in a butterfly net and thought he was a butterfly.' This so exactly described Fred's own condition — a man imprisoned in a room out of which he could easily walk — that Dr Clark felt moved to give a silent command in the name of Jesus Christ for the demon to leave him. That moment a change came over him and the next day he walked out of his room, in effect a different man.

Writing ten years later, Dr Clark records that he was one of the finest spiritual leaders and healers, and one of the most Christ-like men, he had ever known.

4 Epilepsy and Brain Tumour

The following statement was sent to me by an American business man in a responsible position, to whom I was introduced by the late Dr Rebecca Beard, a Quaker lady who had herself been in practice as a doctor but had become a spiritual healer, after having been miraculously restored to health[2] some years before when given up by her medical colleagues. It is interesting as an example of a case in which medical skill seems to have played as much a part as spiritual healing in the patient's eventual recovery.

This man had a motor accident in November 1945 resulting in a compressed fracture of the twelfth dorsal vertebra and slight concussion. The seriousness of his condition was not recognized by the patrol officer who attended to him and he was allowed to proceed to his work. Several hours later he was found unconscious at the desk in his office. It was subsequently discovered that he had made seven lucid telephone calls, though he himself had no recollection of making them. He was taken to the emergency doctor's room. The doctor came to the conclusion that he had had a grand mal attack of epilepsy due to brain trauma following his accident. He was removed to hospital and, after the reduction of the fracture, he spent three and a half months in bed in a body cast.

By October 1946 he was considered to be ready to resume work but, being in pain, he was soon sent home again and back to bed. What was thought to be pleurisy turned out, when he was X-rayed, to be

[2] The account of this is given in the first of three noteworthy books: *Everyman's Search, Everyman's Goal* and *Everyman's Mission* by Rebecca Beard (Arthur James, Evesham, Worcs., and Harper Bros. of New York).

multiple thoracic spine fractures due to the development of osteoporosis through being so long inactive. This new discovery was a shock to him, and maybe that was responsible for another epileptic attack which he had two weeks later. Various remedies were tried without avail and for months the patient went through indescribable torture, though never giving up hope of a cure.

Eventually, in April 1947, a lady doctor prescribed mesantoin, an anti-convulsant, and in a very short time the grand mal symptoms ceased and never recurred, though he had many mild seizures in the form of a sudden lack of physical and mental control. The faith that he would be cured was much strengthened by hearing an address on spiritual healing given in 1949 by Dr Rebecca Beard. Four years elapsed, however, before he was completely healed, and he thinks his cure was delayed because he had to be cured not only of convulsions but also of 'the fear, animosities, apprehensions and a few pet hatreds' he still harboured, and he had to reach the point of forgiving himself for the stupid accident which had started all his trouble.

In March 1953 he began to lose the power of co-ordination of his left side. The cause was diagnosed as a brain tumour by a team of specialist neuro-surgeons. They advised an immediate operation with only a fifty-fifty chance of survival, and in any event they said it was too late to save the use of the left arm and leg. He agreed to have the operation and the tumour proved to be the size of a baseball. To the amazement of the doctors, the night after its excision, the patient was able to move both his left arm and left leg. Physiotherapy was started next day, 24 June, and return to normal was rapid. The doctors had said that he would be confined to bed in hospital for at least thirty days but he was out in seventeen. No pathologist, it was said, had been able so far to classify the tumour, although sections had been sent to several laboratories in different parts of the country. The patient in his letter to me said that he felt he owed eternal gratitude to his good lady doctor and Dr Rebecca Beard for the faith they instilled into his disordered brain when his chances of recovery seemed very slight indeed.

5   *Encephalitis and Infantile Paralysis*

A bishop, on the evening of 25 March 1953, received an SOS that a boy of nine in a preparatory school had been struck down with infantile paralysis and encephalitis. When he arrived at the child's home at about ten o'clock, the family doctor was hanging up the telephone after hearing from the Harley Street specialist, who had been called in, that all would be over in less than twelve hours. However, the bishop knelt down and prayed for the boy's recovery, 'if it be God's will'. At that very hour a change came over his condition. In a fortnight he was out of his iron lung; and he 'is now completely restored, to the awed astonishment of doctors and nurses alike'. These particulars were sent to me by the bishop, chief actor in the drama, as a brief and striking testimony to the power of prayer, though the sceptic is of course free to say it was merely a matter of coincidence and that *post hoc* is not equivalent to *propter hoc*.

6   *Brain Tumour*

Towards the end of January 1946 Mrs B, who to all appearance had previously been perfectly well, suddenly had a stroke. Her own doctor was at a loss to account for her condition and, at the request of the family, a specialist was called in. His diagnosis was tumour on the right side of the brain and he expressed the opinion that there was no chance at all of recovery: in fact, the patient was given only a few hours to live.

Mrs B was now in a state of coma and her relatives and friends, when they heard that she was beyond human aid, formed themselves into small groups to intercede on her behalf in prayer. An Adult School, with which she had been closely associated, was one such group; a Mother's Meeting was another; and some neighbours stayed up all night to pray. Report says that the first few hours left to her seemed endless: 'she hung on to something one felt but could not see, sustained by a wonderful love.'

One week, two weeks, three passed and still she remained alive. Her sister, in a letter to me, records that one incident stands out in her mind. She had left Mrs B's room one morning, while she was still only semi-conscious, when suddenly she heard her beginning to sing a hymn. She sang two hymns right through without hesitating, every note clear, while her sister and the daily woman stood listening spell-bound. Her doctor could not understand how she managed to linger on, and the relatives asked if the specialist could come again to see her. This was arranged, but shortly before he arrived, what the nurses in attendance thought must have been mucus passed from the tumour on the brain through the bowel out of the body. In point of fact a tumour of the brain is unlikely to be mucus and it could hardly find its way into the bowel. What is certain is that from that moment recovery began; the patient regained consciousness and became quite clear-headed, though still unable to use the left arm or leg.

When the specialist arrived, he gave her a very careful examination and she herself thanked him for coming. His response, as he knelt by her bedside, was that God had saved her life, acknowledging in effect that he had been able to do little more than examine her.

Her husband's doctor also visited her subsequently and was amazed at what had happened. Mrs B continued to improve steadily and made a remarkable recovery. Though her left side remained of little use, she could move her leg enough to get into a chair or car and she lived on until 1951, maintaining splendid spirits throughout.

7 Paralysis

An elderly lady, who had just become a widow, was suffering from a somewhat 'distressed heart' and she was sent by her doctor to the south coast. He thought she would benefit from the change if she found a house there. Shortly after getting there she was standing outside an estate-agent's office when suddenly her legs gave way and 'wouldn't work'. She was carried back to her hotel and a doctor was called in to examine her.

It so chanced that the doctor consulted was interested in spiritual healing and was accustomed to seek divine help in the course of his professional work; it was, in fact, he who sent me the details of this case. He diagnosed the patient's condition as paralysis of the legs, resembling in all details a paraplegia of sudden onset. In conversation with his patient he discovered that she was an active Church worker and consequently he felt that it was not out of place to discuss the subject of spiritual healing with her.

They both agreed to pray about her condition and, on his second visit two days later, they had a quiet time of silent prayer together. It transpired that, between the two visits, both patient and doctor had thought quite independently of the same Scripture text, namely, 'This is the way, walk ye in it.' After their time of quiet, the interpretation of the text seemed to them perfectly clear; she knew that 'she should not leave the work she loved most, visiting and praying with sick folk'. So she decided to go back to her old home town instead of continuing to look for a house on the south coast. The return of her legs to their normal state followed this decision in a period of about twenty-four hours.

The doctor added this comment: 'If this lady had been treated purely from the medical angle, she would have been sent to hospital for investigation for tumour, polyneuritis, and other blood infections. I think from other experiences of this nature, that the condition would have become exaggerated and taken many months of hospital treatment with a very slow response.'

8   *Disseminated Sclerosis*

The next case was introduced to me by the friend who gave me No. 12. She impressed me as a very reliable witness. I have also been in touch with the healer who was concerned in both cases, and a few facts about him may incidentally be of interest. He experienced a conversion at the age of 26. Previously he had not thought much about spiritual matters, being self-engrossed and immersed in mundane affairs. Born in the north of England, he had just spent five years in South America and had returned home with the idea of starting a new business. Falling in with an old friend and his wife, who were happily married and who were, as he put it, 'ardent crusaders for the Christ way of life', he was

24

ac 868

carried away by their infectious 'enthusiasm, love and faith'. In his want of understanding of what the call to him really involved, his first thought was to dedicate his new business to God, make a lot of money by it, and then he imagined he would be free to give all his time to serving God.

Possessing no Bible of his own, he bought one and began to read it. There came to him then a burning sense of mission and, in particular, a longing to heal the sick. He began, indeed, to practise healing in his spare time, for he must have discovered early that he had the charismatic gift. He himself maintains, however, that he has no special gift; he says he is simply used as a minister through whom healing flows from God, and that it would flow as readily through any other man or woman prepared to become an appropriate channel for it. Be that as it may, ten years or more elapsed before he became a full-time healer. This followed the sudden and unexpected collapse of his business after the end of the Second World War and since then he has not looked back. He is a man now in his prime and full of vitality, radiating cheerfulness.

I obtained particulars of the case which follows only after some correspondence, and I propose to let the patient tell his own tale. The letter I received from him struck me as being so perfectly natural and refreshing that I thought it would be a pity not to let my readers enjoy it as I did. I have done nothing to it except amend the punctuation in one or two places for the sake of clarity, and I have left blanks or altered the names of persons or places where they might otherwise lead to identification.

The friend who told me about him in the first place reports that his physical condition has improved enor-

mously since he had treatment and she recalls a verbal
testimony he gave at a 'follow-up' meeting that, the
other day, he came to a flight of thirty-two steps which
he had never been able to attempt before and, 'putting
his hand in the Lord's, he found himself at the top
before he knew where he was.'

Here is his letter to me dated 12 October 1953. I
should perhaps say that we are quite unknown to one
another apart from this correspondence.

At last I am going to attempt to answer your several
letters, the first handed to me by my dear friend Mr D
that he had received via . . . , the second and third direct
from yourself. But first I want you to accept my apology
for writing in pencil; it will be much easier for me, as
this will probably be the longest letter I have ever
written, and I fail to see how I can tell any of my story
without telling nearly all. Also, if you will bear in mind
the fact that eighteen months ago I could not write at
all, then I know you will be able to excuse the many
faults this letter will contain.

Now my history. I am 47 years of age. About eleven
years ago I found that I began to fail a little with my
left hand and foot. The first thing I had to give up was
tennis; next dancing. Towards the end of the war I
was running a small dance band for entertaining troops,
Y.M.C.A. clubs, etc.; eventually I found that my left
hand fingering (I played alto saxophone then) was
letting me down and I had to give that up. As the
trouble grew worse and the list of things I was no longer
able to do grew longer, my wife and I went to see my
doctor who then decided to 'open up' and told us he
thought I was afflicted with disseminated sclerosis.
There was no cure for it; I would go on getting worse
and I would finish up a helpless invalid. I might as well
know it and make the best of it, but he would get me

into the ... Hospital just to make sure. During the next year I went into three hospitals, including one in London, but I still continued to get worse and they apparently all finally agreed with my own doctor's verdict.

About May 1952 after I had lain almost helpless in bed for quite a long time, I forced myself to get to my doctor and told him that if they wouldn't do anything more, then I would. He begged me to hang on a little longer and he would contact London again. The result of this was another session in the ... Hospital and this time, with my permission, they tried an operation on my spine, although I was warned it was purely an experiment and I might even be worse after it. They were quite right: I was. That is about the end of the medical history, thank goodness. I can only hope it won't bore you as much reading it as it has been a bore for me writing it; still, you asked for it.

On Saturday, 10 January, 1953, my boy, who has joined a local youth club at the Congregational church, told me that he was reading the lesson at the Sunday evening service the following day, and as he didn't feel too good about it, would I go? I suggested that, if he was going to make a mess of it, surely the less witnesses he had, the better. He replied: 'No, Dad, I'll feel better if you are there; and if I feel too jittery, I can kid myself that there isn't anyone else about and that I am reading it just to you.'

I don't know if you are a parent, D. C. J. If you are, you will know the answer: I went. It was the first time I had ever been to this queer little church round the corner. Well, I ask you? If I had not been able to find God in all the grand churches and cathedrals I had visited, there wasn't much hope of finding Him in one that hadn't got even one stained glass window. Anyway, after the lesson, read quite successfully by the way, a bloke named Mr D did his stuff. The subject: Where

27

to find God? The answer: In your own heart and nowhere else; *really* want Him to be there, make room for Him, and then no matter *who* you are, or *where* you are, God is with you.

I think it was on Friday, 20 February, that although I was supposed to be going somewhere else, I found myself struggling up ... Street to get to the Friends' Hall, where X (a well-known healer) was holding a meeting, and of course Mr D was there. I was quite at my worst when Mr D helped me on to the platform to X, who 'operated' on my arm and then my leg; and honestly, as he prayed for each part of my limbs, I felt the paralysis slowly leave each limb and with him I was able to walk quite normally without my stick all the rest of the time that I stayed in the hall.

And yet, as I walked away from the hall on my way home, I felt that dead feeling coming back into my left side *and I didn't care a damn*, because I knew that in the future anything I really wanted to do — with His help — I could do, and so it has been, and I think will be for the remainder of my life — with His help I can do anything; by my own, well I'm rather a poor cripple.

I have been to another Healing Meeting in my own church since and I did not even ask for help, because I didn't want X to use one minute of his precious time on me, because I *know* — he proved it to me, that if you ask God's help, really believing that He *can* and *will*: He will give it. And so I could not bring myself to occupy one minute of X's time that might mean so much to another cripple who hasn't got the blessing that I have got.

Well, there it is; if you are only interested in my case as a healing, you had better write me off as at least a very doubtful egg. If it's miracles you are studying, I can only suggest that you join quite a group of people and wait and see; as a matter of fact, I am among them.

Really I am very sorry about this letter; it can only be a disappointment to anyone seeking proven facts, and yet perhaps among it all you may find something interesting; I don't know. The following facts, however, I do know:

1. I am back in my job and, although I have not yet managed to do what I regard as a full week's work, each week I do just a little more.

2. That I have never been so happy in my life as I am now.

3. That I would not swap my body for that of the world's finest athlete if he was an atheist.

4. That I am now concluding the longest letter I have ever written.

9 *Asthma*

Mrs E, now (21 October 1953), aged 63, had suffered from asthma since she was 36. She thinks it was due to neglect of repeated colds, but that seems unlikely. Her doctor tried all sorts of remedies, medicine, injections, plugging her nostrils 'with some kind of stuff' on it, but to no avail. She still spent miserable nights fighting desperately for breath. Sick and tired of it all and unable to afford the continual expense, she finally gave up going to the doctor and decided to carry on as best she could.

Early in November 1951 her daughter read in an evening paper that X was coming to their home town on 9 November, to lecture on divine healing by prayer. She decided to go with her daughter to hear him, just out of curiosity to see what he did and how he did it, but with no idea of being healed herself.

They went and she described the scene in a letter to me. The first patient was a man who could not keep his balance; he had to be helped on to the platform and was not able to walk straight. As X laid his hands on his head and offered prayers for him, the man was healed.[3] X walked with him four or five times across the platform and then told him to walk by himself. This he did, walking as if nothing was the matter with him. Mrs E went on to say how this affected her.

> I was spell-bound . . . the inspiration it gave me made me feel I wanted to go to X at once. So I stood up. He had called another woman, but he said he would take me afterwards. It just took me all my time, wheezing and panting, to get to him. As I reached the platform, he helped me up and in a few minutes I was healed. Just imagine my thankfulness to both the Father and X when I came off the platform and walked briskly to my place as I hadn't been able to do for years.

It is two years since this occurred and Mrs E has had no trace of asthma since. She is not the only member of her family who has received benefit through the ministrations of X. We shall have occasion to give the history of the others later.

10 *Bronchial Asthma*

Dr F is in general practice but is at the same time interested in unorthodox methods of healing. He sent me particulars of a patient of his, a girl of 17, whom he had been treating, on and off, for nearly ten years. Her complaint was chronic bronchial asthma, from which she had suffered ever since she was 18 months old. She was seldom free from it for more than a few weeks; she would then be confined to bed for varying periods of time. The longest free interval he could remember her having was two months, and of late, referring to the

---

[3] Whether this cure was permanent we do not know.

year 1951, the attacks had been getting more frequent and more severe.

At Dr E's suggestion this girl went to see Mr Y at one of his Healing Clinics and was treated by him in December 1951. For the next six months there was no recurrence of the asthma; then she had a slight relapse, due to a chill which she caught while on holiday. This last attack was much milder than she had experienced before, and she was confined to bed under Dr F's care. From the effects of the chill she failed to recover and she died of a heart attack, but her parents say that for the six months after her treatment by Mr Y she enjoyed perfect health such as she had not known since early childhood.

11   *Migraine Headaches*

Dr F's wife is described by him as a hard-headed 'down-to-earth' type, Lancashire born and bred, the last person in the world to be cured by hypnotic suggestion and certainly not by faith for, until her cure, she professed none. On impulse one day, watching Mr Y at one of his clinics, she amazed her husband by suddenly jumping up and asking Mr Y if he could do anything to cure her migraine headaches. He ran his fingers down the nape of her neck and remarked: 'Ah, here is your trouble; you will feel no more of it.' She has not needed to go to him since, for the paralysing headaches from which she had suffered for two or three years have altogether ceased, although she does occasionally have comparatively mild headaches due probably to blood pressure. For the migraine headaches she had been sent to hospital before visiting Mr Y; X-ray of the cervical vertebrae was negative and no treatment other than symptomatic had been prescribed.

INFLAMMATORY CONDITIONS

12 *Paralysis and Bronchiectasis*

A young married lady, Mrs D, 25 years of age, was suffering from paralysis as the result of contracting poliomyelitis at the age of two. She was also martyr to a rather intractable disease of the bronchial tubes and lungs, called bronchiectasis. She had been X-rayed by the specialist who first diagnosed this disease, and in April 1953 it was pronounced as too far advanced for operative treatment. It gave her much pain and left her in a very weak state. For the paralysis she was given medical treatment up to the age of about ten, electric and hand massage, and exercises; also she had two operations in these early years. Since the age of two she had worn many different types of iron caliper on her right leg.

A friend who had been interested for some two years in divine healing, and who claims not only to have read about it but to have herself both seen and experienced its results, spoke of it to Mrs D. As Mrs D had given no thought to the subject before, this friend lent her two books about it and took her to a Healing Service on 6 May 1953. She was undergoing no medical treatment at the time which could account for any change in her condition when she went forward for treatment.

The healer first treated the serious lung condition by placing his hands on her chest and praying aloud. As this was done she felt new life pulsating through her body. She breathed deeply and was free from pain. She then mentioned the paralyzed leg on which, as always, she was wearing a caliper. He passed his hand down the leg and prayed. When Mrs D mentioned that she had come prepared with a pair of shoes with no caliper

32

attachment, he immediately helped her to remove the caliper and to put on the other pair of shoes. He then encouraged her to walk up and down the aisles. She did so as she had never done before. Cure was instantaneous. She had a feeling of elation, a tingling in the leg and a sensation of heat. Also the leg felt strong and she had a longing to use it actively.

Since that day Mrs D has had amazing energy. Her friend told me that 'she is studying to be a Methodist local preacher and the beautiful spirituality of her nature was a great help towards her healing'. The cure has been lasting. One leg, however, is as yet shorter and slimmer than the other and there is a stiffness in the ankle movement. Since her healing she has been learning to ride a bicycle. The lung condition is completely cured. She has been X-rayed by the specialist who diagnosed the bronchiectasis, and he could find no sign of trouble but expressed a desire for another X-ray in three months. Her own doctor found an immense improvement in the lung condition when he examined her on 14 May. He noted also the change in the leg but about this he made no comment, though her friend and she 'sensed a suppressed excitement'.

A letter dated 19 October 1954 states that the leg which had been in a caliper now appears to be the same size as the other, but a slight limp still remains. There has been no need for another X-ray as Mrs D is in excellent health. The account here given is based on the patient's own statement and the evidence of the friend who accompanied her when she was healed and was in close touch with her throughout.

13 *Chronic Sinusitis*

The next case comes from Dr A, who gave me the

second in my series. He takes an unusual personal interest in his patients. Not only does he treat them professionally but both he and his wife with a small group of friends have their needs prayerfully in mind for more or less lengthy periods of time, depending on the severity of their condition. He told me that, while he believes in the almighty power of God and in the sufficiency of His grace for all needs, he does not believe that He will always heal, even in response to our passionate desires and our strong faith in Him. 'Thy will be done' marks the limit and 'His permissive will may involve for us suffering and disease'.

One of his recent patients was a man of about 40 with a septal defect and chronic sinusitis. He had been operated upon during the war by 'an over-zealous and under-skilled service surgeon' and was left, in fact, 'suffering from a surfeit of surgery', as someone more skilled described his subsequent condition. He used to be off work for months, nearly always in pain and at times almost suicidal. He was accustomed to see Dr A two or three times a week. In addition to much surgical and medical treatment he was seen and prayed for by a spiritual healer of some repute. Dr A and his friends were also praying, not merely for his physical healing but that he should find spiritual comfort and come to a real faith.

When these prayers had been offered on his behalf he became literally a new man and, dating from that change, he had little or no further pain, was back at work and put on weight. Prior to this there had been no sustained improvement in his condition. Writing to me more than two years later, Dr A reported that he now only saw this patient once or twice in twelve months. The physical deformity of the nose and air sinuses was still present but he was suffering no pain or inconvenience from it. In short he was certainly keeping sufficiently well to require no medical aid.

14 Disease of Middle Ear

My next case concerns a friend of mine who had suffered for several years from disease of the middle ear. This weakness had become apparent some fifty years ago. She had been obliged to leave school at 13 years of age in order to nurse her parents, and her subsequent condition was attributed to the strain of nursing. The early symptoms were bad ear gatherings and relief came only when the gatherings burst. The ears were syringed from time to time under advice from the doctors who attended her. As a result of the gatherings the drums became perforated, but new drums grew in their place. These, however, were so thin that the syringing had to be discarded, and in any case it had produced no lasting beneficial effect.

We now come to 1951. During the last six or seven years of her disability there had been in addition a continuous discharge from one ear, sometimes excessive. Various experiments were tried by the specialist who was treating her to alleviate the condition, including drops, penicillin powder, and cauterisation. How far they were in any degree successful it is impossible to say, but certainly there was no significant reduction in the amount of the discharge; and even as far back as 1940 she had been assured that there was no permanent cure and that she was too old for an operation.

In the spring of 1952, however, the conviction suddenly came to her that this discharge was, literally, 'matter in the wrong place', and from that time a noticeable improvement began in her condition. This definite change of attitude towards her disability led her also to pray that complete healing would follow, and there came to her a sense of exhilaration and a strong belief that her prayer would be granted. Hitherto the most she had asked was that her condition should not interfere with her work and it had never done so. She had led a very busy life, after her parents died, in such posts as helping to train subnormal children, looking after mental patients, and acting as a school matron.

She herself belongs to a Prayer Group interested in divine healing, and I asked if her group or any other had prayed on her behalf. She said no, she had a great reluctance to allow her name to be placed on such a list. This I could appreciate, for she is a lady of great independence of character. Moreover, her attitude was to this extent justified, in that the discharge from her ear ceased within a week after she herself had prayed for complete healing and, apart from a slight return after an interval of more than two years, there has been no trouble since. Her final visit to the hospital was on 13 August 1954, when the specialist said he was satisfied that there was no activity in the ear and, very gratified, discharged her.

It should be added that, soon after the initial healing in February 1952, her doctor had made an appointment for her with the specialist for another cauterization, and she felt it right to keep it, for she considered that it was probably all in line with the healing process. Incidentally her own doctor at that time was as delighted as she was with the improvement she was able to report, but she formed the opinion that the doctor's faith was in the treatment she (the doctor) and the specialist had been prescribing rather than in divine healing. She herself added this characteristic comment: 'Never mind, if the

Lord chose to use her drops, what of it? I am quite content to let that be regarded as part of the healing process. I feel I should prefer it not to be miraculous and sudden. My faith in myself does not face up to that kind of experience.'

15 Varicose Ulcer

A lady, herself in medical practice, had a very bad varicose ulcer of the leg, which refused to heal though she tried a great many ointments, U-V rays, etc. Occasionally it improved a little, but always relapsed. Then she decided to try the healer Mr Y whom she knew and believed to be 'entirely sincere and unworldly and always ready to help'.

The treatment was to be absent treatment conducted at a distance, not in the presence of the patient. She admits that she was no doubt using some kind of dressing when she applied to him for help but, as already mentioned, no dressing had previously done more than alleviate the condition of her leg. This time nothing happened for two weeks; then the ulcer began to improve and within a couple of months the leg 'was healed and has remained so to this day'. That was on 1 May 1952, and when she wrote to me again on 14 October 1953 she was able to confirm that the cure had lasted.

16 Sycosis Barbae

This same doctor gave me particulars of another cure by absent treatment. I record them in her own words, written 27 April 1952.

A patient came to see me about ten years ago suffering from sycosis barbae: a very intractable skin disease caused by using an infected razor blade. For eight or

37

nine weeks he had received no proper treatment, not through any fault of his, but owing to a variety of causes too long to explain here. When at last he consulted a skin specialist, the latter told him he would do his best but that, as he had had no proper treatment for nine weeks, he would be lucky if he were cured within nine years. He was treated by various specialists and, though sometimes the sores seemed to be healing, they always broke down again.

At that time I had known of one or two cases that had been cured by Mr Y and, since I could suggest no other remedy, I suggested to my patient that he should write asking him to give him absent treatment. 'It sounds absurd,' I remarked, 'but, after all, this condition is a severe handicap to you, and even if the treatment fails, it can do you no possible harm.' He knew nothing of psychic healing and seemed sceptical, but finally he agreed to do as I suggested. About a month later he came again, and it was obvious that the sores were healing. 'But this has happened before', he said, 'and they always break down again.' He agreed, however, to keep in touch with me, and about five months later he called to see me. The sores were completely healed, and there was nothing to be seen but a certain amount of scarring. He did not live in this neighbourhood and I did not see him again, but he wrote about six months later saying that there had been no recurrence. A couple of years later I heard from a friend of his that he was perfectly well.

Since sycosis barbae is a contagious, very intractable complaint, this seems to be clear evidence that certain persons *can* heal at a distance without even seeing the patient. You ask for only one case, so I will not trouble you with others, but I have known of other equally convincing cases, which have dispelled my disbelief in some kind of power possessed by certain people, of whom Mr Y is an example.

17 *Persistent Rash*

The youngest daughter, aged four years, in the family of an architect (see Case 33), was troubled with a persistent rash and spots, supposed to be due to food allergy. Ointment was applied intermittently over a period of two months, by the doctor's direction, when the irritation became violent. The irritation abated when the ointment was used but the spots remained. Then prayer was offered and one of the parents laid hands on the child while she was asleep, with the result that the rash and spots disappeared overnight. This happened nearly two years ago and there has been no return of the trouble.

18 *Tuberculous Knee and Eczema*

Miss K came to England from Johannesburg in 1898 when she was five years old, and within two or three months she began to be seriously troubled with eczema, owing, it was thought, to her blood thickening too quickly with the change of climate. The eruptions were very bad in the spring and autumn, when her arms were crippled with pain.

At the age of 20 she fell in the garden of her home and hurt her right knee-cap, with the result that tuberculous trouble rapidly set in and the leg began to waste above the knee. The family doctor in consultation with a Harley Street specialist, prescribed first a plaster splint, then an iron one; finally a fibre splint was found to be most suitable because it could be moulded to fit the shrinking leg.

Two and a half years after her fall three different specialists advised sending her to a hospital by the sea. There she remained for nine months, when she was transferred to a nursing-home in the same town. As there was no improvement in her condition after the lapse of some weeks, she was taken home, and she never left her bed for six months during that winter season. Then sun treatment was tried for eight months but without avail, so that too was dropped.

Miss K spent long hours at needle-work to keep her mind occupied and to forget the pain. In 1925, however, she began to suffer from eye-strain, the pupils filming over, so she was obliged to give up her needle-work. The following year a change was again tried: she was moved to the house of a married friend in London where she remained for nearly a year, but there she fell a victim to influenza. A fresh doctor was called in to see her and she was persuaded to let him examine her knee. He pronounced the knee-cap to be entirely destroyed and said she would never walk again. 'Then you can give me no hope,' said she. 'No hope whatever,' he replied emphatically. At this same time her home doctor was advising Mrs K to have her daughter's leg amputated, but this she resolutely refused to consider.

The effect of the London doctor's verdict was to cause the patient gradually to collapse in despair, and such a serious view was taken of her condition that her friend wired for her mother. When her mother arrived, not only was Miss K temporarily blind but her throat was paralysed so that she could not speak; but she has a half-conscious recollection of her mother kneeling by her bedside and praying aloud for her recovery. She lay thus for six weeks literally hanging, at first, between life and death, but in course of time her mental condition improved and she returned to full consciousness.

At this point in her story a letter came from her sister to say that a revival campaign was being held in her home town; not only were conversions taking place but wonderful miracles of healing also, as in the early days of Christianity. Miss K told me that all her family had faith that, if she could only be taken to one of the meetings, she too would be healed; but she herself was without any such hope. However, a week later she was prevailed upon to make the journey from her friend's house to her home town, and a very risky and painful journey it was. In fact it was taken entirely against the doctor's orders and for the next five days she had to stay in bed.

She was taken to her first revival meeting on 4 May 1927, although there happened not to be a divine healing service that evening. She was so ill that they were afraid they would never get her there and, when they arrived at the hall, she was very nervous at the thought of facing the crowd whose singing she could hear, for she had not been inside a church half a dozen times since she first met with her accident fourteen years before. But the man at the door literally lifted her carriage off the ground, up the steps, and into the hall. Once inside she says she felt the presence of the Lord Jesus and she lost her fear of the people. After an address on the Christian's disappointments, which seemed to describe vividly her own experience, came the hymn: 'All hail the power of Jesus' name' and, during the singing of that hymn, faith came to her that she would be healed.

She was still very conscious of being in the presence of God when she was taken home. She was 'lifted up indescribably in prayer' and she cried repeatedly: 'Lord, if there is anything amiss in my life, take it away, and let me be healed for Thy glory.' That night of prayer she counts as the secret of her healing. The next day she was again carried to the meeting. The missioner had asked the previous day how long she had been 'lying in this old carriage'. 'I haven't walked for fourteen years,' she said, 'it is a wasting disease.' 'Do you believe the Lord can heal you?' he asked. 'Will you come to the Healing Meeting tomorrow?' To both questions she had answered 'Yes.' On the second day he repeated his question: 'Do you still believe the Lord can heal you?' 'Yes,' she said, 'but my leg is in a splint.' 'Never mind the old leg,' said he, 'you just believe and pray.' And he himself prayed: 'O Lord, turn back the disease, unlock these joints.' As he said the word, she felt a tingling warmth surge through her body. A Wesleyan deaconess who was present in attendance testifies that the carriage shook, and Miss K felt her knee, which had been rigid for fourteen years, move in the splint. She was so far healed instantaneously that she was able to step out of the carriage and begin to walk, the missioner guiding her steps. She had not the least pain at the time in any part of her body, and although her leg was still in the splint, she felt as if she were walking on air.

It was shortly after 4 p.m. when she got out of her carriage and the hall was still full of people at six o'clock, so she was taken to the deaconess's room while the hall was cleared. When she got there her sisters unlaced the splint, and she stood up and prayed: 'Now, Lord, I am going to walk without the splint.' She got only as far as the door and back to the chair. The leg, though healed from actual disease, was too thin and weak to bear the weight of the body. When they tried to lace up the splint again they could not do so, because the leg above the knee which had wasted to be like a baby's leg had already begun to thicken.

She was pushed home in the carriage, but she walked

into the house and immediately took off the splint; she also removed the bed-cradle which had protected the leg from the weight of the clothes. The foot which, during the years of illness had been icy cold, was now warm and comfortable, and Miss K slept through the night, the first time for many years. An examination by daylight the next day showed that all trace of the eczema had also gone and her sight had been fully restored. Moreover, the leg which had shrunk in the splint began to grow again in the course of the next morning as Miss K walked in the garden, although it remained about half-an-inch shorter than the other for about twelve months and the knee was still stiff. She records also that she ached all over on the second day after the healing from the unaccustomed exercise.

The healing had taken place on a Thursday and her friends urged further prayer for the bending of the knee, but she was not prayed for again at a public meeting. On the following Monday, however, while the family were singing after supper, Miss K began to pray and her example was followed by her mother and sister. As they prayed she states that the knee-cap began to form and it continued to do so for twenty minutes. She was in such agonies of pain while this was in process that the perspiration dropped from her face and hands.

On Easter Monday 1929 a Harley Street specialist, consulted as to the completeness of the cure, made a thorough examination of Miss K and certified as follows: 'There is not a trace of tuberculosis in the body anywhere. The knee-cap is normal in every particular and perfect in every movement.' The last letter I had from Miss K, in January 1954, states that she has now for some years been in perfect health and leading a very active life in the church with which she is associated.

43

19 *Chronic Osteomyelitis*

Leonard, a university student of divinity, had been suffering for several years from osteomyelitis of the leg. The disease is similar to an ulcer in the bone; pieces kept flaking off the main bone and the treatment consisted of scraping the affected part. The patient had been attending hospital for this repeated scraping operation but the leg grew worse rather than better. It broke down every six months and he was feeling very despondent about it.

In January 1949 he was again in hospital awaiting another bone scraping, when through a friend he was visited by an experienced healer connected with church circles. Leonard described to me what happened during his visit:

> He knelt down in one corner of the room and I was sitting in a wheel-chair, having been brought out of the ward to see him. Suddenly my head was lifted up. At first I thought that he had come across to me but, on opening my eyes, I saw that he was still on his knees in the opposite corner of the room. Then he did come across to me and placed his hands on my forehead and gently rubbed. A quivering came right up through my body. A bright light shone on my eyes making them smart and a wind blew in my face. After this I became very tired and went to bed. My wound dried up immediately. I told the specialist but he just didn't believe me. He got me up on crutches, but I did not need them, and the next morning I went round the ward collecting the eggs for the patients' breakfasts.

A doctor at the hospital kindly turned up for me Leonard's case-sheet. It recorded the diagnosis of his trouble as chronic osteomyelitis of the leg, which had been treated with penicillin and operation, but there

44

the medical notes stop. The fact remains that, until the visit described above, there had been no apparent progress towards recovery in the patient's condition and that after it he was discharged as cured. This was confirmed by another friend who knew Leonard and wrote to me about him. By the autumn of 1951, when I last heard from Leonard himself, he said that he was again playing cricket and rugby football after a lapse of fifteen years.

20 *Nephritis*

Dr Leslie D. Weatherhead, minister of the City Temple, London, has kindly given me permission to use this case. I do not propose to go into the full particulars as they will be found elsewhere.[4] David, aged about three, was lying seriously ill in hospital with inflammation of the kidneys, and his mother, who used to be a member of Dr Weatherhead's church in Leeds, wired on 25 January 1948 to ask if his congregation would pray for David. Intercession was made every Sunday evening until mid-March and people also prayed for him privately.

On 11 February the mother wrote to say that all the doctors agreed that the kidneys were permanently damaged and that David would never be the same again. Subsequently he was sent home from hospital and

[4] The full account will be found in Dr Weatherhead's book, *Psychology, Religion and Healing* (Hodder and Stoughton, 1951), which is the most readable book I know as a first approach to the serious study of Spiritual Healing. Several other books have been written in recent years on the subject but with rather a different purpose, usually laying stress only on its devotional aspect. I have not considered it necessary to provide a bibliography since, by application to any of the organizations interested in spiritual healing, a list of such books would be readily obtainable.

it was clearly expected that he would soon pass into a coma. The ward sister had said to the mother on the day he was taken home that she was glad his mother would have him for the last few months.

On 24 February came the wonderful news that the kidneys had unaccountably begun to work again. No drugs had been given since his life had been despaired of. The sequel is best told in a letter from a doctor:

I am enclosing the hospital report which embodies that of a very excellent specialist, Dr ———. In this report you will observe the very serious nature of the case and the unfavourable prognosis.

The boy was suffering from a very serious form of nephritis. After his return home from hospital he did not make any progress at all in spite of very careful treatment. I have attended a number of similar cases and *never saw one recover*, and owing to this and the absence of any sign of improvement, I could not give any favourable prognosis to the parents which would allay their deep anxiety. One day which I shall always remember the father asked me if there was any hope at all for his recovery, and I had to reply that, as far as I could see, there was definitely no hope whatever.

Within about a week after this, David's condition had completely and suddenly changed for the better, and in a very short time he was practically normal which was most extraordinary to me.

You may quote my remarks in any publication you wish.

21 *Poisoned Kidney*

Early in January 1940, the wife of a clergyman was taken seriously ill a few days after the birth of their second son. The trouble that had developed was a badly inflamed kidney and her condition was such that the young doctor in attendance had her removed within a few hours by ambulance to a nursing home. Her husband had been away from home, but he got back that same night and reached the nursing home at about 9.30 p.m.

The specialist was reputed to be the chief surgeon in that part of England. He had only delayed operating until the husband's return, so as to get his written authority to proceed, and he expressed surprise when the husband hesitated. 'Young man,' he said, 'your wife has not got a kidney, only a bag of pus; if you do not let me operate, you will not have a wife.' The husband replied: 'I am in your hands but give me time to get prayer help.' On this the surgeon, evidently somewhat irritated, commented: 'I am the son of a clergyman, but I have given up all that nonsense long ago.' He then paced the room and, striking the table, remarked that he always operated on a Friday and he had not lost a patient yet; he was prepared to operate before midnight or sooner if the matron called him. The clergyman then said: 'You are not religious, but I see you are superstitious.' This annoyed the surgeon; but he listened to the explanation given to him that 'touching wood' was a superstition, based upon touching the Cross, and reluctantly he consented to the husband telephoning SOS. messages to his friends for help in prayer. The husband on his part signed permission for the operation should the surgeon think it imperative. Only on that condition could the wife remain for any length of time in the nursing home. However, before midnight, the kidney started to function normally again, with the result that no operation was performed.

The wife stayed on at the nursing home for ten days under close observation, because she was anxious to retain milk for her baby. She was then allowed to go home on the understanding that she would return there again after six weeks for a thorough overhaul; and she was in fact able to feed her baby when she got home. When she went back for examination on 29 February four distinct tests were used, and no trace of blood-poisoning in the system was found by any of them. She was not wholly under the influence of the anaesthetic during this examination and she recalls the specialist exclaiming, with mixed astonishment and satisfaction, at the healthy state of her kidneys; in fact, he said after-wards that, judging by their condition then, there might never have been anything wrong with them.

All this took place fourteen years ago and the lady tells me that she has had no recurrence of inflammation of the kidney, although she has since had occasional bladder trouble but not recently.

CASUALTY SECTION

22 *Slipped Disc*

Dr F (see Case 10), in 1948, had acute pain in the lower back which was diagnosed by a specialist in neurology as a slipped disc. He was admitted to hospital under the care of this doctor and was confined to bed for four weeks. He was then discharged as being apparently quite well. Two years later, as a result of a heavy fall, the disc slipped again. Signs and symptoms were exactly the same as before but much more intense: the least movement caused the most intense pain.

At his wife's suggestion Dr F phoned Mr Y at his home and he was given an immediate emergency appointment. Getting there was a painful process but it was eventually accomplished. Mr Y passed the fingers of his right hand down the patient's back over his clothes; beyond a slight swaying movement there was no attempt at manipulation of any kind. The acute pain disappeared at once and Dr F got up and walked, without help, up some steps. A dull ache, all that was left of the pain, was cured by two subsequent treatments a few days later. Nearly four years later he reported to me that he had had no return of the pain.

Dr F informed me in one of his letters that he had heard that a number of Mr Y's alleged cures had been followed up and evidence of curative action was said to have been found in only about four per cent. of them. The test, he understood, was to X-ray the patients and, if the slides showed no change in their condition, the conclusion drawn was that the change must have been in their imagination only. On the other hand if the patients themselves not only felt better, but continued to feel better, after treatment by Mr Y, the evidence of the slides could surely be discounted. As Dr F shrewdly went on to remark:

If Mr Y cured only four per cent of his patients, do you think for one moment that he would be besieged by the thousands who flock to him as they do? Remember that in almost every case his clients are people who have been told by doctors that no more can be done for them. They have turned to him or to some other healer in desperation. What sort of figure do you think that I, or any other doctor, would cut if faced with such a clinic as Mr Y faces twice a week? Could we by the mere laying on of hands unlock joints that have been locked for years or straighten spines that have been bent since birth? All these and more I have witnessed at his clinic.

E 49

The healer whom I have called Mr Y might be thought to be on rather a different footing from that of other healers whose cases are recorded in this book, being in the nature of a spiritualist healer. But he himself has said that with all Christian religions 'one discerns as the necessary essential for the healing of the sick the common factor of the sending forth of a thought force (prayer).' And he adds that the spiritualist healer also prays to the Infinite Spirit for healing to take place. In a guide to any who may wish to develop the gift of healing he has said that their first thoughts should be prayerful ones addressed to the Father of all mankind.

From this and the examples given of his method of treating patients, it is clear that his approach to the problem of sickness does not appear to differ essentially from that of others who are termed spiritual healers, and he evidently goes to the same source for inspiration and power in his ministration of healing.

23 *Curvature of the Spine*

A Durham coal miner, George, in the middle forties, had worked at the coal face for a number of years and had later served as store keeper and deputy. He had had slight accidents at various times when working at the coal face; for instance, a piece of stone once fell on his back; another time he himself slipped on an icy slope and his head hit a concrete step.

In October 1948 George was off work for six weeks and was treated by the doctor for rheumatics. He was again off work for a few weeks at a time in the following two years. In August 1950 the doctor sent him to the infirmary to get a proper diagnosis of the recurring trouble, which was judged to be probably due to an accumulation of what at the time did not seem to be very serious incidents. At the infirmary he was treated at first for a sprain for five weeks and then he was X-rayed. In October four different doctors diagnosed his trouble as curvature of the spine due to osteo-arthritis. George was told that nothing could be done to put the spine right, but he was ordered to wear a saddle-type spinal jacket to keep the spine static. He received it in January 1951, and in March the Resettlement Board found light work for him in a garage. He became absolutely dependent on this support. Often on a Sunday morning he would sit and read until meal time with it off but, when he attempted to move, he found he could only struggle across the room in a bending position and in terrible pain.

As a lad George had attended a Methodist Sunday School but later in life, when he was nearly 40, he became a Christian Spiritualist. One Tuesday evening in July 1952 he was talking to a number of people in the C.S. Church, of which he was President, when a lady visitor gave him a copy of a devotional journal containing particulars of many who had been healed through the ministrations of the healer X. Having read it overnight he thought it might create interest in his church if X were invited to come there and conduct a Healing Mission.

X came a month later and took two services. About 200 people were present at the evening meeting; many testified to spiritual help and not a few to physical benefit. X said he was willing to stay behind at the close of the meeting at nine o'clock, if any others present wanted healing, so that none should be disappointed. Almost everybody stayed on and the missioner was kept busy until 10.30. George was one of the last to go forward to the patients' seat. X placed his hand on his spine and prayed, 'not asking, but thanking God for His wonderful gift to me. Even then I was not sure but, on rising from my seat, I raised my hands above my head, leaned forward, touched my toes, and again straightened up without pain. Thank God for the great deliverance, I was free. I took off my support that same night.'

All medical treatment had ceased in January 1951 when George got his spinal jacket, because the doctors said they could do nothing more for him. Hence their treatment could hardly be claimed as contributing to his cure. The cure took place in August 1952 and was complete, for it was tested by George carrying bags of coal and other heavy weights up the stairs on his back, and he has had no recurrence of the trouble.

In October 1952 George moved from County Durham to another coal field and he has passed the medical examination to work again in a coal mine. On re-starting he was put to coal hewing, but, after twelve years' interval from doing any heavy work, he found working at the face too heavy. He therefore asked for a lighter job, so he is now engaged on the night shift clearing up in the pit bottom. In his spare time during the day, when not resting, he does painting, decorating, and sign writing, and is thus kept constantly busy. He mentioned this in his last letter to me to prove that he has really tested his cure and fears no recurrence of the back trouble.

24 *Curvature of the Spine*

Miss Heaton, a young woman of 24, was knocked over by a car which had got out of the driver's control when she was riding a bicycle down a busy street in Norwich on 6 March 1931. She was taken to hospital and, on recovering consciousness, she found herself lying in bed. Two strange men were sitting beside it: the son of the man who had knocked her down and a friend. The son said he understood she was not hurt very badly and he offered her £5 to be going on with. In her dazed condition she assented and also signed her name to what turned out to be a compensation insurance document.

While in hospital her legs were X-rayed. The damage done to these and other cuts were healed after one week and she was discharged as fit. But, as soon as she got on to her feet again, her spine and ribs began to give her pain. She told her doctor and he bound her ribs, which gave relief; but she returned to him again and again about the pain in her back. He advised her to try to forget about it; so she gave up complaining and went back to her work as a dressmaker, making model dresses in a large shop. But she found she could not forget the pain; it prevented her from working well and sometimes she had to return home on account of it. After two years she was obliged to give up going to the shop altogether and work at home instead. The work was brought to her by a friend with whom she lived, who was also a dressmaker. So the time passed; mostly she lay in bed but occasionally she was wheeled out in a chair: not often, because it was more painful.

Two years later Miss Heaton had lost the power of standing and her legs began to give way under her. If she sat she could not keep upright; the shoulders fell forward. During all this time she was not seen by her own doctor, but now a friend persuaded her to see another doctor. He ordered an X-ray examination and a damage to the spine was discovered: the curvature was stretched to breaking point. This was in 1938, seven

53

years after the accident. At the hospital they began to
try to straighten the spine by manipulation, electrical
heat, massage etc. Gradually spondilitis set in around
the injury, causing excruciating pain. She was told she
must give up her work and stay in bed for a year to get
relief. So she lay in hospital having every care and
attention from doctors and nurses; but they were unable
to do anything for her except relieve the extreme pain
by morphia injections.

When war broke out in September 1939 she was
finally judged incurable and sent home as one disabled
for life, with a pension of six shillings a week and £5 only
as compensation for injury. The description and interpretation of what followed is given mostly in her own
words though put in the third person. Feeling that she
could not possibly go on living in this miserable condition, Miss Heaton began to prepare for the end. But, in
the meantime, God's Holy Spirit was stirring to life a
desire within her to reach out to Him. There followed
an intense search for God, which began with reading
the story of Jairus' daughter. She sent in turn for her
minister, her class leader — being a Methodist, though
lukewarm in the practice of her religion — and her
doctor, but none could help her. The minister, though
kindly, evidently thought she had 'one foot over the
border'; the class leader advised her to lay down her
Bible and read a light book; the doctor scarcely cheered
her by saying that, if she moved, there was a danger that
her spine would snap.

In desperation she prayed that God would guide her
to Himself and that He would make known to her anyone who today was healing the sick as in Christ's day.
The very next morning a friend called to see her and
left with her a book by Hugh Redwood. Turning the

pages her eye caught sight of a case of spinal healing from the case records of the Rev. Howard Cobb, giving the address of the Home of Divine Healing which he ran for twenty-two years at Crowhurst in Sussex — after having himself been cured of sleepy sickness — until his death in 1951.

Miss Heaton shouted to the friend who looked after her that God had answered her prayer. The friend came upstairs and wrote, at her dictation, a letter to Mr Cobb, asking if he would help her to get to know Christ so that she could seek healing direct from Him. The result was that she was taken to his home. His first words to her were 'You want to find Christ, don't you? Well, you can't find Him but He can find you.' Then followed journeys full of adventure through the Bible in his company. He taught her about the Holy Spirit and about sanctification, salvation and redemption, so that the word of God came alive to her. Never a thing on either side was said about healing. In fact, looking back, Miss Heaton thinks she lived above the body. She slept well and cannot even recall whether she was in pain. She was kept warm and clean and she was always anxious to get rid of maids and nurses so as to get on with her study of the Word. She could not remember what she ate, for she went on all the time through meals with her reading and thinking.

Her attention was focused on God and the silence of her room helped her to concentrate. She was taught by the indwelling Spirit which led her into truth and, when she came to know truth, to understand God's word, she was set free. She believes that her body was set free at the same time. As she put it to me: 'What you attend to or concentrate upon, you bring into your life.' She forgot her infirmity; if she was to die in six months, what did it matter? She would leave her body behind. So she began to be filled with a sense of peace and harmony. It is possible to forget the body and its suffering if God is really present. Everything is transformed in the light of His presence.

Six days after her admission to the Home she felt so conscious of Christ's presence with her and so full of peace and joy that she told Mr Cobb of it. He too was overjoyed and said: 'Now you can ask for healing.' But there was nothing to ask for: healing had taken place. Having become one with Christ, she was made anew. The sister in charge was fetched and passed her hand down her spine, pressing it where it had been nearly severed, and said it was perfect; the hump which had developed on her shoulders was also gone and she arose healed in soul and body. She walked straightway down the garden and presently sat up at the table for lunch. When she went into the doctor's surgery a month later, 'he was humble enough to say he had tended me, but God had mended me, and a perfect miracle had happened'.

Miss Heaton's healing took place in February 1940. The same afternoon she walked over two miles to the parish church to give thanks to God for His goodness. To this day, fourteen years later, there has been no recurrence of her trouble.[5]

25 *Curvature of the Spine*

I owe two most fruitful introductions to Dr J, a missionary doctor serving in India, whom I found to be thoroughly reliable and cautious in his judgment of men

---

[5] Since this was written the full story has been published in a pamphlet under the title *The Face on the Wall* (Arthur James, Evesham, Worcs.).

and matters coming within his professional field of observation.

By him I was put into touch with Col R, Professor of Medicine and Medical Superintendent in an Indian Medical College; and with Bishop Q, referred to by Dr J in the following terms: 'most particular about working in with doctors and nurses as far as possible and I have great confidence in his observations and methods of work. He has been used by God in a wonderful way in the ministry of healing.' My next case comes from the bishop. Others due to him and Col R are recorded in Part III.

Miss I was born on 4 November 1915. When in boarding school at the age of 13, it was noted that she was developing spinal curvature. Her left hip protruded outwards and a hump appeared on her right shoulder blade. Owing to domestic trouble she was not taken to a doctor until 1930. He ordered corrective exercises, electric massage, sleeping with a weight under the right shoulder blade, and the wearing of an iron jacket or, as a change, cloth straps. This treatment did good, but after about seven months Miss I failed to persevere with the exercises; also the electric massage was given up on account of the expense.

She still had curvature and the hump early in June 1933 when prayers were offered for her and she was anointed, with the laying of hands, by Bishop Q. She attended preparation classes daily before the Healing Service. She described this service as a wonderful experience; for a whole week after it she felt 'a supreme spiritual uplift' in which she 'seemed to see Jesus in everything'. Her spine, too, was somewhat strengthened and, at the bishop's request, she began to take more trouble with her exercises and to wear her iron jacket again for part of each day. As a result there was an improvement over the next ten years, although a doctor who examined her spine in 1935 had said that nothing could be done for it because the bones had hardened. This was confirmed in 1943 when, at 28 years of age, she was taken to another doctor who gave her a careful X-ray examination.

From 1943, probably as a result of this judgment, Miss I slackened off again in her spinal exercises and gave up the iron jacket. The same bishop anointed her a second time in June 1944 and the large hump is said to have gradually disappeared, though the spine grew weaker and she was becoming more helpless through physical exhaustion. She records the fact that she attended Healing Services in 1950 and 1951, when she felt 'bathed in currents of love and power', bringing temporary relief from her extreme weakness. But in July 1952, during a three days' unbroken chain of prayer, she had a sense of being 'finally strengthened by the Divine touch on the spine, making it truly like iron'. She felt not only that she was completely healed but that she would remain healed. She was 'a new being, moving as if winged', and she was 'able to walk and to enjoy walking for miles'.

In a subsequent letter, received towards the end of January 1954, she added a qualification and clarification of the last quoted statement: 'These currents did give me a sense of completeness and of complete healing and also that I am still being healed. I feel that, so long as we are in this mortal flesh and frailty, we do need and shall always need healing and strengthening, just as we constantly need the Holy Communion, which is God's great gift for the strengthening and refreshing of our bodies and souls. . . . Now and then I still feel a bit weak, and when tired my hip tends to lapse a bit to one side, but thank God He has healed me much and He is still healing me.'

26 Broken Neck

A woman of about 33 had a bad hunting accident in 1935 and she has kindly sent me full particulars of what followed. Not until eighteen months later was she free from pain and able to carry her head properly. She should have been taken at once to hospital and X-rayed, but she made too little fuss because she was 'longing to ride again, pain or no pain'. As it was, she simply rested at home for ten days and then insisted on getting up. The only treatment she had was from a clever osteopath for a few months.

After eighteen months she was able to live a normal life until the autumn of 1951, when she began to have agonizing pain in the head, neck and ears. Why this long delay in the onset of pain is not explained. An X-ray examination then revealed that the neck must have been broken in 1935. The medical view was that she was now too old to have it reset. Various methods of treatment were tried without success, including 'hanging' in hospital twice weekly for a few weeks, which eased the pain for a time, but it returned as badly as ever and the patient was still unable to turn her head properly.

Having read in the *Science of Thought Review* of the success of a certain healer, she wrote to him and made an appointment to go to see him on 22 August 1952. She was in great pain at the time and barely able to hold up her head for more than a moment or two. Only then did he learn of the broken neck, and that her trouble appeared to be due to two of the vertebrae at the back of the neck having become joined together, as shown by the X-ray plates.

The patient was treated lying face down on a divan, while the healer stood behind her head. Placing both hands on her neck, with the fingers resting along the spine, he called aloud on the life and power of Jesus Christ. No pressure was exercised and no attempt whatever at manipulation was made. He just kept his hands resting along the spine and, according to his own statement, tried to hold his whole 'being completely open and receptive to Jesus Christ and His mighty healing power'. Within a few minutes he seemed to feel a slight movement under his hands, as quick as a flash of lightning, and almost intuitively he knew that the work was done.

He moved away and asked the patient to get off the divan. As she did so, she was astonished to find that the set of her head on her neck was different and all pain had gone. She cautiously turned her head from side to side and realized that she could now do so with ease and safety.

A few weeks later she had occasion to visit the physiotherapist who had previously given her manipulative treatment. When she demonstrated to him the complete freedom, strength and control she now had in her neck and told him how her healing had occurred, he admitted that no physical treatment could have done it and that it was nothing short of a miracle.

This case was reported in the *Science of Thought Review*,[6] December 1952, where it is said that the woman's entire outlook on life is now different. 'Instead of feeling that life is one long, grim struggle against

[6] Published by Science of Thought Press, Chichester.

frustration and difficulty, she now finds herself full all the time of gratitude and praise, and at the same time newly conscious of wonderful peace and love.'

27 Injury to Coccyx

In June 1936 John Fraser, who was in the army, had a bad fall and injured his coccyx. He was not X-rayed immediately after the accident; in fact, he had no treatment other than a short period of rest. He had pain from it but this did not become severe until 1938, when he suffered sadly from arthritis in the sacral region and sciatica in one leg. In March of that year he was X-rayed and operated on. A piece of bone was used as a kind of splint to fix the lowest three vertebrae of the spine. The intention was to prevent the pinching of the sciatic nerve, but it was not a success; the effect was to move the sciatica from one leg into the other and his back continued to give him considerable pain.

Mr Fraser was discharged from the army on that account and also because he fell ill with pneumonia and peritonitis. From these he recovered but the pain in back and leg persisted for years, until he went to see the same healer that was concerned in Case 26. The date was 2 October 1951. He told his story and was placed to sit on a chair. The healer put his hands on his head, asking at the same time that healing might take place. Mr Fraser then lay on a couch and the healer went through the same process, placing his hands on the patient's back and asking for healing. The patient's reaction can be given in his own words: 'I must admit that I expected something tangible to happen, some sort of demonstration — that I could see — of something taking place. Nothing of that kind did happen though I felt considerably uplifted. A week later I went down with a high temperature and my face was covered with blotches.'

He went for his second treatment after a fortnight had elapsed. The same procedure was followed and again, apart from the same mental upliftment, without any visible or physical result. A week later he records that he felt very, very tired and, after the lapse of another fortnight, he went for his third treatment. This time he says 'I felt a warm glow pervading my whole back and pain ceased from then.'

The healer himself reports that Mr Fraser had 'a slight relapse due to indulging in unusually strenuous activity'. This was about two months after his third treatment; it cleared up immediately with one more treatment and the patient had no further trouble.

In reply to the question whether he was having any medical attention during the time when he was visiting the healer, Mr Fraser replied that he had not been near a doctor since about May 1950. Nothing was done for him then, except that he was given a surgical corset to wear. He told me also that, when he first visited the spiritual healer, he 'hadn't a clue as to what sort of thing he did' and he was far more nervous than when he went to see a doctor. 'In fact', he said 'I was hoping that I might miss my bus so that I could have a good excuse for not going at all, but I was not allowed to do that. And I use the word "allowed" because I am quite sure that, once I was "pointed" in the right direction, I was under the guidance of Someone who knows all the answers.' In one of his later letters, he adds 'Not only was I cured physically, but mentally as well. My whole outlook on life changed and I became conscious of God being all around me, and I now feel that I am on talking terms with Him.'

28 *Fractured Skull*

A friend, knowing of my interest in the subject, sent me a press cutting telling of the remarkable cure of a boy which was claimed to be the result of prayer. The boy was said to have been attended in hospital by one of London's leading consultant surgeons, whose name was given with that of the hospital. I was so struck with the contents of the article that I wrote to ask the surgeon whether he could confirm or correct the account given in the paper, explaining the object of my inquiry.

The surgeon was hesitant at first but, on my assuring him that I did not intend to publish names with my records, he was good enough to send me the following details of the case.

> The boy's age was 6. He had fallen thirty feet from a balcony on to his head and sustained a severe fracture of his skull. He was unconscious for 14 days and, on regaining consciousness, he had lost the use of his legs and was deaf, dumb and blind. No operative treatment of any kind was carried out, but united prayers by the patients and staff over a considerable period were answered by a gradual return of the boy's functions. After a period of six months he was able to walk, see, hear and speak.

In the account given in the paper it was stated that the boy was back at school. It also gave further information of interest about the surgeon. He believes he has had such wonderful results in his work by seeking God's help that he has urged his colleagues to do the same. He told them, at a private medical meeting in London, that before beginning the rounds of each orthopaedic ward, he leads the patients in this simple prayer:

O Heavenly Father, Giver of life and health, we

thank Thee for all the varied forms of Thy divine healing power, and especially at this time for the work of the doctors and nurses and the wonders of medical science. Hear us now, we beseech Thee, for all who are sick in this ward. Stretch forth Thy hand to restore them to the fulness of life and health. Bless with wisdom and skill the doctors and nurses, that Thy healing power may flow through them richly to all who are sick.

29. *Injury to Back*

This is another case sent to me by Dr F, who has been mentioned before as concerned in Cases 10 and 22. In May 1951 a woman, just over 50 years of age, fell heavily, with the result that there was a severe contusion of her back in the mid-dorsal region and to the ribs of the right side. She was confined to bed for several weeks as a result of shock and fibrositis of the muscles. Although no bones were broken she was in so much pain at times that the doctor had to give her opiates to induce sleep. When she was able to get about again, she had frequently to rest after walking a very short distance on account of the pain in her back.

Dr F visited her every day at first after the accident and then weekly. She then attended one of Mr Y's Healing Services, held at a Congregational church, on 12 December 1951. She sat in acute pain in the church, but it went the moment Mr Y laid his hands on her, and since then she has been quite free of it both in the back and ribs. She was subsequently treated by Dr F for a fibrositis of the right arm and shoulder, described by him as 'a comparatively minor sequel'. This had also cleared up and she still felt no ill effects from the accident when he last reported on the case on 14 November 1953.

30   *Cracked Pelvis*

The next case to be considered is that of Oliver, the youngest son of Mrs E (Case 9). He was a taxi-driver, working for a private firm, and in 1948 at the age of 25 he had a drunken fare who argued over the charge. Before Oliver was aware of anything, this drunken man had dragged him off his seat, knelt on him, and had hold of his throat. Oliver managed to get out of the taxi and the man kicked him twice and he dropped. Two men at this point came to his aid and took him to the infirmary, while the drunken man was taken in charge.

Oliver did not work any more for a long time, as he was suffering from a cracked pelvis and paralyzed bladder. He was given disablement pay and nine shillings a week pension and he had periodically to pass medical boards. The doctors used to put on his paper 'retention of urine', and when he was in difficulties a male nurse was sent to attend him. Also, he would lose the use of his legs and had to go about on crutches. Eventually, with his mother's help, he got a car and started taxiing on his own account. But, when he felt his old trouble coming on, he did not drive until he was better.

Some four years after the above described attack, on a Wednesday, 30 April 1952, Oliver was engaged in mending his car when he was struck by lightning. His left side was paralyzed and he lost his sight. The doctor who was summoned could do nothing for him and sent him the next day to the infirmary. After he had been there $4\frac{1}{2}$ hours they said they could do nothing for him either, as they had not had a case like that before. So he was taken home on a stretcher and put to bed again.

In the meantime, on the Wednesday night, his

mother had telephoned to their friend X, the healer, and told him of their trouble. He replied that it was her opportunity to 'keep that light shining'. He too would pray for Oliver. On the Friday morning, when she was still in bed looking through a book which X had just sent to her, the daughter-in-law looked in and said, 'I am bringing you a surprise.' So saying, she led in the son on her arm. They got him downstairs and his wife began to read to him out of the same book. Presently he began to move his arm and then he began to walk; but he had to feel his way, for he was still blind. On the Saturday morning, as they sat together after breakfast, Oliver's eyes began to water and his mother thought he was crying. But that was not so: he said they burned and smarted, and when that was over he could see perfectly.

It is necessary to explain here that X had not been told of the drunken man's attack on Oliver four years previously, but one day in August 1952, the son had driven his wife and mother over to a meeting at the Mission Centre and they stayed on afterwards to have tea with X. It so chanced that the son had a return of his old weakness and his legs suddenly gave way under him. X naturally asked what had happened and the whole story came out. X then remarked: 'The Father made you perfect, so He will make you perfect again'; and he laid his hands upon Oliver there and then and offered a prayer for his recovery. The result was that he did immediately recover and has been quite well ever since. He subsequently worked for the British Road Transport Service but now he has a bread-van round.

31 *Smashed Thigh*

We now pass on to the next case in the same family.

Oliver's little girl, aged six, was knocked down by a car coming from behind a stationary bus, on 25 March 1953. She was in a very bad way, her life hanging in the balance, and she was given a blood transfusion. Her thigh was smashed and she had to have twenty-one stitches in her face. Her leg was set and put into plaster, but the plaster was removed later because it had the effect of making one leg shorter than the other; consequently the shorter leg had to be stretched. The family at once telephoned to X about her and from that time she began to improve. Young as she was she seemed to have surprising faith in Uncle X. When her granny said that 'Uncle X has asked Jesus to tell the good doctors to make your leg all right soon, and then you can go to see him at . . . and they will give you a wonderful time. That will be nice, won't it?' She replied 'Yes, but my Uncle X is cleverest.'

All the doctors, the matron, and nurses were amazed at 'how well she had come through'. They said she was the best little patient they had ever had at her age. On 17 April she was well enough to be taken home, hardly more than three weeks after the accident, whereas the doctors had said it would take a long time. She was still in plaster, however, from chest to toes and was to continue so for three months.

Writing early in June her granny reported that the little child remained in plaster only for one month and she went about on crutches for a further three weeks. She had been taken by car to see X and to be 'treated' by him on 28 May. Although one leg was still three-quarters of an inch shorter than the other when she left the hospital, her granny, writing on 20 July, said that shortly before writing she had noticed for the first time that the child was walking without a limp; and in a later letter, 21 October, she recorded that her healing was quite perfect; she said 'You would not know that there had been anything the matter with her.'

32   Broken Pelvis and Ruptured Bladder

The history of this case was given to me by Peter and it relates to his brother Ralph, who was on his way to work on his motor-cycle early on 2 June 1948 when he collided with a five-ton motor lorry. He had a friend as pillion passenger. Both were thrown under the lorry, the rear wheels passing over them, and the friend was killed.

Ralph lay still, thinking that he must pray and not move, to avoid further damage to his broken limbs. He prayed, saying that he had many times boasted of the Lord's power; now he needed that power more than ever before and he asked God to bless him. A doctor chanced to be following the motor-cycle when the accident occurred. He was amazed to find both men alive though he could see that the friend would not live more than a few minutes. After attending to him, he gave Ralph an injection and ordered his removal to the nearest infirmary. Ralph knew his friend had died.

Peter and his father went to the hospital at about 10 a.m. and saw Ralph in bed. A surgeon had examined him and ordered a blood transfusion and an X-ray photo to be taken to ascertain the extent of his injuries. Ralph was conscious and told Peter how the accident happened. He added that he was not going to worry and asked Peter to go for his wife and mother.

The hospital sister told Peter that Ralph's injuries must be very serious, that he was dangerously ill and that the surgeon would probably operate when the nature of the injuries was known. They proved to be a broken pelvis, ruptured and punctured bladder, broken ribs and superficial knocks. His wife, mother, and father were with him until he went into the operating theatre at about two o'clock. His mother said to the sister 'Do all you can for my boy.' She replied: 'If God wills, he will get better. We will do our best.' A second blood transfusion was given to him just before the operation and a third just after, at 4 p.m. The doctor said 'He is very, very seriously ill, but he is strong.' Further than that neither he nor the hospital staff would commit themselves.

Peter's uncle, a Methodist local preacher like Ralph and Peter, had spoken by telephone to the hospital sister and formed the opinion that recovery was hopeless. Peter — with the uncle and their minister — returned to the hospital between 5 and 6 p.m. Ralph, though dazed, seemed very cheerful. The minister went in first to see him and offered prayer for him. The uncle and Peter afterwards went in. He told Peter he felt much better and, seeing his uncle, he said: 'Hello, Uncle; yes, I'm afraid you'll have to preach for me at . . . on Sunday.' His uncle replied that of course they would be helping him all they could, and Ralph commented: 'Yes, these people don't know how much can be done by prayer.'

Returning to his home base, the minister told the details of the accident to the Methodist Quarterly Meeting which was being held that night, and many prayers were offered on Ralph's behalf. Peter went to his parent's home. The mother's reaction was 'If Ralph's work on earth is done, he will die; if not, he will live.' All the family spent much time in prayer; even Peter's little boy, aged seven, said his prayers more urgently than usual and afterwards said to his father: 'Dad, Uncle Ralph will get better, I know,' so helping to confirm Peter's faith in his brother's recovery. Ralph's wife and mother spent the night at the hospital and a nurse was on duty all night with him. She too was a Methodist and spent much time in prayer for the patient's recovery. In fact, it is true to say that prayers were offered in the churches, and by friends in the congregations in the neighbourhood, that night and many succeeding nights.

On 5 June Ralph's condition shewed improvement, though the doctor and nurses would only admit that he was holding his own. He was given a little food, but that upset him. They were worried about this at the hospital and prayer was offered at home about it. The disturbance to his condition ceased the same night. Two days later the doctor was concerned because Ralph was spitting up a lot of blood. An X-ray was to be taken the following day to find out the cause; but again prayer was offered and the bleeding stopped, so that no X-ray was needed.

From that moment progress was steady and sure so that, in eleven weeks and three days after admission to the hospital, Ralph was discharged and able to walk a little. By 14 October he had so much improved that, in about a fortnight, he intended to start work again. At his last examination the surgeon stated that his recovery was such that there should be no after effects and eventually he should be perfectly well again. The doctor who had been at the scene of the accident saw Ralph on 24 September and was amazed. As he shook hands with him, he said 'You are a wonderful man.'

Peter added that the doctor and nurses had all been wonderful; it was impossible to praise them too highly, 'but we all feel that the prayers of God's people helped to bring about this miracle of healing.'

As a postscript to this account, which was written shortly after his brother's recovery in 1948, I can give later information received in 1952 which came in a letter to me from Peter. Here is the relevant paragraph: 'My brother has made a complete recovery; of that I think there can be no doubt. Admitted he has had an operation recently for hernia, which may have been partly caused by the accident, but he made a rapid and easy recovery from that operation. I understand that he had to have an examination some time ago by a neutral doctor for an insurance policy — rather a large one — and that examination revealed nothing to cause the Company to put on any extra premium. He has also changed his job and been accepted by the I.C.I., who, I think you know, insist on a medical examination. Also, apart from the odd cold, he has not been ill at all other than as mentioned above since the accident.'

33 *Broken Mastoid Bone and Sprain*

The next record concerns Quintus, an architect, aged 35 in 1953. Quintus suffered from anaemia, supposed by the doctors to have been due to living, while in the R.A.F. during the war, for two years at a height of about 5000 ft. directing bombers by radar to their targets. This made him appear to be lazy; he would get up late and take chances in hurrying to the office, with the result that on two occasions he had accidents on the road. On the first occasion he was knocked over by a British Railways lorry in January 1952, and suffered from a broken mastoid bone, lacerated foot and delayed concussion, which only revealed itself some months later and resulted in the second accident.

After the first accident Quintus came round in the hospital casualty room, smothered in emergency dressings, at about ten on a Monday morning, having been unconscious for about an hour. He was transferred to one of the hospital wards an hour and a half later, and received no further treatment until about 11.30 on the Tuesday morning. When the time came to change the dressings, the nurse was horrified to find that the wounds had not been cleansed. Apparently the Sister assumed that this had been done already in the casualty room, while those in charge there had left it to be done in the ward.

Quintus belongs to a Prayer Group, most of whom are on the telephone, and in an emergency word is passed round from one to another immediately. The few who cannot be rung up are notified at once by post. The result is that at least half the group 'can go within a few minutes into the Silence, corporate though apart', and within twelve hours ninety per cent. of the group are informed. This was what happened following the first accident to Quintus.

Recovery was rapid; there were no complications of any kind and he was discharged and placed on the out-patient list within forty-eight hours of admission to hospital. I particularly asked if the description of injuries received was as given in the hospital. The answer was 'yes' and it was confirmed by his own doctor, with the exception that there was no evidence of concussion when he was examined in hospital. I suggested that the mastoid bone injury might have been mentioned per-haps only as a possibility at the first inspection, and that on a more thorough examination it proved mis-taken. But Quintus said that the expression used was 'hole broken in mastoid bone,' and he remembers the sister remarking that, 'if the the blow had fallen two inches either way', he would have been killed outright.

In fact he still carries the scar and indent of the pit dug out of the mastoid bone.

Quintus's second accident occurred in May 1952; he fell over an obstruction in the pavement which he did not see. It appears that there was a restriction in his field of vision, resulting in an inability to see below a certain level, attributed by the doctors to the delayed effect of the concussion suffered in the first accident in January of the same year. By slight head movements and corresponding adjustment of the eyes he could bring things into correct focus most of the time, so that previously he had not been aware of his disability. It was only discovered when he went before a Medical Board at the request of his employers.

After his fall he managed to limp to the office, there he collapsed and was taken by ambulance to the same hospital as before. They strapped him up and discharged him, evidently concluding that there was not much the matter with the leg, for they told him to exercise it by walking. He succeeded in getting home but, in the meantime, his leg had become badly swollen between the foot and the knee. His own doctor was then called in. He was openly critical of the advice and treatment given at the hospital. The ankle and calf were sprained and the ankle bone chipped, according to him, and he prescribed hot fomentations and rest.

Owing to domestic difficulties there was a delay of about twenty-four hours before any of the Prayer Group heard of this second accident and most of them did not hear for forty-eight hours. The patient was able to walk, and the sight defect was corrected also, within four days after prayer and the laying on of hands by a healer who works in association with the group. Quintus soon felt so fit and well in fact that he wanted

73

to return to duty, but his doctor would not let him; he said it was too soon and he imposed the full length of sick leave. There had been no subsequent ill effects when the last report reached me from the patient in mid-January 1954.

34 *Fracture of Shin Bone and Scratched Eyeball*

Quintus has a daughter, aged 10 in 1953, the second of three young children. He and his wife have also adopted a homeless baby boy who, in swinging his arms in play one day, caught this little girl's eye with his finger-nail. The scratched eyeball gave her intense pain. The accident occurred at about 3.30 in the afternoon on a day in June 1951. As the inflammation and pain grew steadily worse, the doctor was called in and arrived at about ten o'clock the same night. He treated the eyeball with cocaine. This gave relief for about a couple of hours, after which the pain started again. The parents then got into touch with some members of the group, including the one who ministered to healing by the laying on of hands, and relief from the pain was immediate. I asked whether in this case it was conceivable that the cocaine contributed to the cure. The father thought not, because the pain had returned as soon as the effect of the cocaine wore off. The doctor called next day to give further ameliorative treatment; he was surprised to learn that the child was at play in the park, and he was not satisfied until she had been brought to the surgery for him to see the eye himself.

Six months later the child had another accident. She tripped over a low skipping rope, left by neighbours tied across their common flat-balcony, and sustained a double fracture of her shin bone. The limb was cased in plaster and again the Prayer Group were informed, this time within half-an-hour of the accident. Recovery was rapid and the child walked two miles into the country fourteen days after the fracture. The hospital authorities were pleased and encouraged her to keep on exercising her foot. In this case the quick healing is attributed to the co-operative effect of prayer and the medical treatment. There has been no recurrence of any trouble since in eye or limb, according to a first-hand report received in January 1954.

35 *Carpal Bone Fracture*

Mr Richards met with an accident on 6 October 1936, through a heavy door blowing against his right hand, an X-ray showing one of the carpal bones fractured. The hand and wrist were temporarily strapped and, two days later, a plaster was put on and he was ordered to keep his hand in a sling for a fortnight.

On 30 October the plaster was cut off and he was instructed to go next day for ray and massage treatment. When the masseur began on his hand, the pain was so great that he said the fracture had evidently not healed and, if he continued operations, he would do more harm than good. He therefore rang up the doctor about it and the doctor decided to renew the plaster for another two weeks. At the end of this period a second X-ray, by an independent radiographer, revealed that there was still no unity. The doctor, on receiving this report, said he could do no more and he made arrangements for Mr Richards to see a specialist, who was the chief orthopaedic surgeon at a well-known hospital.

When this specialist had examined the two sets of X-rays he ordered a new type of plaster, recently invented by an Austrian, to be tried. This was applied on 13 November and was to remain on, with frequent reinforcements, until 2 December, when the patient was to see the specialist again. Another X-ray was taken on 30 November and sent to the hospital. When Mr Richards went for his examination two days later he was seen by the specialist's deputy, who gave instructions for the plaster to remain on since there was still no sign of the fracture joining up. The date fixed for the next consultation was 6 January 1937, five weeks later, and a further X-ray was taken just beforehand. There was still no unity; the treatment was therefore continued and, after a fifth X-ray, Mr Richards was to see the surgeon on 4 March taking all the plates with him.

The surgeon examined the series of X-ray slides and then instructed the nurse to cut off the plaster very carefully and bring it to him. This done, he also examined the patient's hand and said that, as there was still no sign of the fracture mending, the only thing to be done was to open the hand and insert a silver plate. After strapping it very skilfully, he ordered the patient to see him again on 10 March to make arrangements for the operation.

It is not surprising that Mr Richards went away from this interview feeling very depressed, and he made up his mind there and then that nobody should open up his hand. The first thing he decided to do, on getting home, was to ring up a well-known priest who ministered to people in need of divine healing, and ask if he might see him as soon as possible. There happened to be a service in the Lady Chapel that evening and the priest promised to see him after the service. At the interview he said that he would give him the laying on of hands at five o'clock on the following Saturday, 6 March. This in due course took place, and Mr Richards remembers the priest saying one thing which struck him forcibly. It was this: 'The world's standard was to see first and believe afterwards, but I was to believe first and see afterwards.' He tried to keep that thought constantly in mind, and he says that on the following Tuesday afternoon, 'I had a sensation of Power pouring into my hand, and from that moment I knew I was completely recovered.'

On the next day he was to keep his engagement with the surgeon, with a view to arranging for the operation on his hand. The surgeon very gently took his hand and Mr Richards said to him: 'It is all right; it is better.' He said: 'It can't be better'; and he asked him to bend his hand, which he did. He then said: 'Open it,' and he did so. He still did not believe him, so he began himself to work the hand in all directions, and he could not understand why the movement was not causing Mr Richards pain. He then asked him what he had been doing. It was not an opportune moment to give an explanation but Mr Richards wrote to him on his return home.

Under instructions from his own doctor, no doubt following a report from the specialist, he attended the surgery two days later to make sure that everything was in order. Mr Richards adds this postscript: 'Although my hand had been in plaster for six months, was swollen, blue and ill-looking, it was not necessary for me to have any massage, and it is a hand of which I am justly proud.'

CONSTITUTIONAL ABNORMALITIES

36 *Club Foot*

Teddie was born on 25 October 1945 with his right foot imbedded in or twisted on to the leg. The doctor diagnosed it as a club foot. By a series of massages and by stretching the tendons, some progress towards normality was made.

The baby had been taken when he was three months old to the altar of a church, where the rector laid hands on him and offered prayer for his healing. Subsequently he was taken each week to a Healing Service in the same church for about two months.

When the time came for him to walk, both the foot and the leg, from the knee down, turned in toward the other leg. The doctor recommended a cast to be applied and later on braces. The child's mother, however, told me that she decided instead 'to turn to the Great Physician and give Him entire charge'.

She reports that healing was gradual but complete without any medical treatment. The leg and the foot grew to be perfectly normal, so that it was impossible to tell which foot had been affected. She returned to the church to give thanks for his healing and she also took the child to see the doctor. His comment was that she certainly had a lot of faith to believe that no treatment was necessary and, had he been his boy, he would certainly have either put him in a cast or put braces on him. She took the child again, when he was seven years old, for a complete physical overhaul and the medical verdict was that he was perfect in every detail.

37 *Pernicious Anaemia*

I heard of Mrs C through a friend who knows her well and I entered into correspondence with her. In 1942, at the age of 47, she had been lying in hospital in Scotland for six months, a victim of pernicious anaemia. She told me that she had always been very pale and bloodless. Five doctors who examined her gave her no hope of recovery as her blood count was very low, twenty-four when it should have been round about sixty-five. She left hospital for home in July, apparently with nothing to look forward to but repeated injections to keep her alive.

The need for injections was at first very frequent, one a day, because the body used it up so quickly, but gradually she was able to do with only one a week and latterly one a month. This steady recovery she herself attributed entirely 'to prayer and living near to God, the Holy Spirit, both in mind and body'. Her blood count in a period of two years, 1942 to 1944, rose from twenty-four to normal, although the spleen appears to have been permanently damaged. At first she could never lie on her left side without gasping for breath, but in course of time she was able to do this also.

By 1946, her blood count then remaining near the average, she succeeded in doing without the injections altogether, and this remarkable recovery, in November 1953, had lasted for seven years, so that it is not unreasonable to class it as permanent. Mrs C tells me that she has never needed a doctor since the date of her last injection, October 1946.

38 *Gall Stones*

Particulars of this case were given to me by the patient's daughter, Miss I (see Case 25). The mother was suffering from gall stones. The trouble began in 1935, when on and off she was very ill. In 1937 she had a severe attack of jaundice and was taken to hospital, where she had an X-ray examination and was told that she had 'a quarry of stones' in her. She improved wonderfully in hospital and was able in due course to go home, but she was asked to come back for an operation on the doctor's return. To this she demurred, and she was told that she was not to send for the doctor, when she was sick again, if she would not stand the operation which he advised her to undergo. Mrs I did not go back to the hospital and, not very long after, she heard from a friend of some pills prescribed by a doctor which had relieved her friend of gall stones. The same doctor prescribed these pills for Mrs I. She took them in January 1938, and they had the effect of softening the stones and ridding her of them in about two months' time. It is not likely, however, that they would have prevented the formation of fresh stones.

The bishop and a circle of friends prayed for her at the same time and she had had no more attacks of pain and sickness up to the end of the year 1953. The doctor marvelled that, as the years went by, Mrs I did not return to him. If ever they met, he would anxiously ask after her health. 'He himself was a good Christian doctor,' she added, 'and he acknowledged that he believed much in the power of prayer which had healed her.'

39 *Prostate Gland*

Mr M, a man of 65, sent me the following account of his experience. He was having prostate gland trouble, as many elderly men do. This was in the year 1947; it had started five years before, but was getting steadily worse and was now giving him much distressing pain. He had been taking medicine for about three years and going to see his doctor every month or five weeks but, as the condition deteriorated, he was obliged to go every week or ten days.

In early September 1947 the doctor said he was going

to try a newly discovered medicine which should be of great help to him. But it proved to be of no help whatever, so that finally the suggestion was made that he should see another doctor to verify the diagnosis with a view to an operation.

It was at this stage that the thought of spiritual healing flashed through Mr M's mind, and he asked a minister visiting the church he attended if he could tell him by whom and where, in that town, services of healing by faith were held. This led to correspondence with the Rev Dr P, who was responsible for conducting these services. He told Dr P that he wanted God to clear up three infirmities for him: 1, Taking His name in vain; 2, Prostate gland; 3, Hernia. Whether the hernia was also giving him serious trouble is not stated.

A helpful reply came to his letter, together with a booklet on *Religion and Health*. Mr M began then to be troubled with doubts as to whether his sins would not be an obstacle to his healing, and he prayed to have these doubts removed. It was then impressed upon him, seemingly in answer to his petition, that he should go and explain the whole concern to two or three Christian friends and ask them to pray for him. This done, his doubts left him and he felt free to attend a Healing Service on 4 December 1947. The Rev Dr P preached a short sermon and, after prayer, invited any in the congregation to come forward and kneel at the altar for the prayer and the laying on of hands. Mr M went forward and Dr P went down the line, offering the same short prayer as he laid his hand on each head in turn. As he was just approaching him, Mr M tells me that he himself prayed: 'Lord, I know You have the power to do this, to heal me; I will ask You to do it for me.'

At the time he says he felt no sensation of any kind, but by the next morning a complete change had taken place; everything in connection with the gland trouble was removed, and urination was perfectly free without any pain. That was six years ago and there has been no return of the trouble.

After waiting about three weeks Mr M called to see his doctor. He said nothing about his healing until the doctor had examined him. He then asked him if he noticed anything different, any improvement in the size of the prostate gland. The doctor said, No, he thought it seemed to be about the same as usual. Mr M then handed him one of 250 copies of a letter he had written to Dr P, testifying to what had taken place at his Healing Service, and he added that he proposed to distribute these copies among his friends. To this the doctor replied: 'Why, it was the last medicine I gave you that made this great improvement in your condition; this healing business is something that transpired two thousand years ago when Christ was here on earth.' Knowing the doctor and his family very well, for they attended the same Presbyterian Church, Mr M remarked: 'You wouldn't want me to go and tell your mother what you have just said to me; for, after taking your two different medicines for about three years, you advised me to go to hospital for an operation, and now you are claiming that your medicine cured me.' Having said this he walked out of the room and closed the door, for he said he felt very disappointed in the doctor. He thought how much finer it would have been if he had been quite honest with himself, with God, and with him. Happily he has never needed to return to him for medical attention since then, although he remains on friendly terms with him.

40 *Prostate Gland*

An elderly Quaker, well-known to me, described how in January 1948, when in his eighty-eighth year, he was in extremity with water trouble. Apart from this he said he had much to feel thankful for, though of course the infirmities of old age were becoming more and more noticeable. The doctor urged him to be taken at once to hospital for an operation. But this was a serious step to contemplate at his advanced age, and he expressed a wish to leave the decision open until the following morning. This was granted reluctantly by the doctor, who later confirmed in a letter to me that the diagnosis had been enlargement of the prostate gland and retention of urine.

Recording his experience some time afterwards, the old man said:

My wife that evening supplicated that, if consistent with His will, and He had more for me to do to witness for Him, that He would be pleased to heal me; but if not, that He would give me grace to bear what He might see fit to lay on me. I also desired that, if the chastisement was needful for my good, some other form less distracting might be permitted instead.

The next morning I had faith given me to tell the doctor that I desired to see what the Lord would do for me first. The woman in the Bible had spent all that she had, and had to come at last to the Fountain (Christ). I preferred going there first.

The doctor thought we were taking a great risk. But, without any means or remedies, I soon began to mend and in three weeks or less was as well as I need be, blessed be the Lord, who is yet able as of old to do great things.

On 11 December 1953 I heard from his wife that he

83

was still mercifully quite free of his old trouble. In fact, in his 93rd year, he was said to be wonderfully well, apart from the action of the heart which was not as good as it had been.

41 *Glandular Dystrophy*

Miss N, a teacher of biology and a local Methodist preacher, aged 30, interested in the interaction of science and theology, has kept an unusually objective diary of her healing experience. She had been under treatment for $4\frac{1}{2}$ years for thyroid and pituitary glandular dystrophy, taking three grains of thyroid, three grains pituitary, and two or three tablets of benzedrine each day and being given two injections of antuitrin S each week. The symptoms were exhaustion and very low blood pressure; also the usual increase in girth, not natural rolls of fat but the definite hard bulges associated with pituitary thickening. She had had an accident when she was 19, the base of the skull being damaged causing concussion. The head was X-rayed and the report mentioned unusual calcification in one so young. At 21 an ovary was removed. The thyroid symptoms were observed when she was between 25 and 26.

Early in 1953 Miss N heard of a Healing Mission that was coming to the town where she lived. She says she was highly sceptical about the laying on of hands and, although she joked about it once or twice, it never entered her head to try for healing that way herself, because she thought she would have been healed in the past if she could have mustered enough faith. The consequence was that, although she attended the Mission, she went out of mere curiosity to see if there was anything in it. The conduct of the service impressed her very favourably, but she still thought people would receive only spiritual benefit from it; whether healing came afterwards would depend on their faith. She prayed very little, being intent mainly on observation during the service. But the conviction slowly dawned upon her that she herself ought to be at the rail. This conviction grew stronger the next day as she discussed the matter with friends, and she began to make tentative arrangements with that in view after a fresh reading of the Gospels on the subject.

On the following Sunday evening, 8 February 1953, she again attended the Mission Service and herself went forward at eight o'clock to the rail, feeling no emotion and no stirring of faith, but believing that she was obedient to God's will and hoping more than anything for spiritual healing. When the missioner's hands touched her neck she felt a deep-seated burning, not diffuse but concentrated in an area of irregular pattern. The heat was 'uncomfortable and slightly strangling' and unexpected, in that it was not 'dorsally at base of skull', where she thought she would feel it when the missioner's hands were laid there.

Miss N returned to her seat without any feeling of spiritual 'uplift'. The burning sensation lasted all evening, at first in the thyroid gland region, not on the surface of the skin and neck muscle. The heat spread slightly to the left in the thyroid region and, later on, it lessened there and spread up strongly to the tonsils. Then it lessened there and passed up the left eustachian tube to the left middle ear. There was still a slight sensation of heat in the ear the following morning. Taking a meal had not affected the heat in the throat the previous night, and by 11.30 p.m. the tonsils, which had been very enlarged, were surprisingly smaller.

Going back in her record, Miss N says that she was

conscious of better blood circulation after returning to her pew. Also, following two hymns, she noted a backward jerk in her shoulders, beyond her control, the position of the lower part of the body remaining unchanged. There was no movement in the waist, only in the region rather more than half way up the thorax; she felt as if a noose round the neck was pulling her head upward. Suddenly there was a more violent and prolonged pull and a straightening out of the vertebral column. She could feel the vertebrae grating but there was no pain from the stretched muscles. This movement was quite unexpected, as no-one had ever mentioned spinal curvature as one of her afflictions. It is not surprising therefore that she admits to feeling 'a bit light-headed and somewhat scared'. Walking up the street after the service, she had trouble in keeping her shoes on: her feet were definitely not so podgy.

Although she stopped up late on that Sunday night, Miss N says that she felt much fresher when she awoke the next morning. She needed no strong cup of coffee, her normal early morning drink to help her get fully awake. Her head was much clearer, as if a load had been lifted off her brain. Her shoulders have not gone back to their original position. During the morning she smoked as usual but she did not take her first dose of benzedrine, thyroid and pituitary until lunch time.

During lunch, at about one to one-thirty, her head and neck suddenly jerked up again. She could not get them down, so she left most of her dinner 'owing to unusual eating position'. She took no more drugs that day. Her head remained clear and, after an exceptionally heavy day, she felt tired but not so desperately tired as she normally felt by early afternoon. She was in bed by 10.30 and relaxed for the first time. Stretching movements began again when she relaxed, but she found she could now stop them.

On Tuesday she took one dose only of her tablets, her head being clear. On Wednesday she took two doses, and in the afternoon had to take aspirin for a severe headache, which may have been due to too many tablets or to a special visit of H.M. Inspector at her school. She lay on her bed in the afternoon and the stretching started again, the whole spine being affected this time, expecially in the lumbar region.

On Thursday the spine was still straight and her shoes loose. Also, near the end of a Fellowship Meeting, she felt the heat sensation again but this time in the small of her back. Later it travelled up the spine and settled at the base of the neck. It was still noticeable at eleven at night after walking a mile in cold air. She suddenly realized too that her left leg, affected by an old injury, no longer ached when she walked quickly.

Miss N reports that, one month later, she felt her blood pressure to be higher. Her back was still upright, especially at the neck and waist, her feet were no longer swollen and there was no pain in her leg; her hair was softer, she could walk indefinitely and quickly even up hill, her clothes did not fit owing to the change in her figure; and all this time she had taken no tablets, needing neither them nor injections.

In a letter to me, written 10 October 1953, eight months after the healing took place, Miss N said that most of the healing occurred the first night and spread out over the following week. Recovery did not yet appear to be quite complete, as her health continued still to improve. Asked if she was receiving any medical treatment at the time of healing which might in some measure have accounted for it, she replied that the tablets she was taking merely served to prevent the symptoms from increasing. Previously she had tried reducing the dose of drugs taken but found that she always had to return to the full quantity. They did not, and were not expected to, effect a cure.

There had been no relapse in the eight months' interval from February to October. Occasionally, when depressed, she has thought it might be the beginning of a relapse and she has begun to take thyroid-pituitary again; but it was clearly not necessary, for it played havoc now with her blood pressure. She used to be a very heavy smoker, but that too she has had to modify, because she finds it sends up her blood pressure. Incidentally, her hair which was red has become definitely darker, tending to auburn in colour.

Her doctor, when he saw her after her healing, at once agreed that there was an improvement in her condition. He was pleased but non-committal; he no doubt wanted to be sure that the improvement was likely to be permanent.

42   *Haemorrhage*

An American lady, over 70 years of age, early in 1948 began to have occasional bleeding from the womb. She had had nothing of the sort before since cessation of her menstrual periods and she was at a loss to account for it. But, as it was accompanied by no pain or illness, she was not at first alarmed by it. However, as the condition continued for some months, she decided to consult her niece about it, who was a reputable physician with a large practice.

The niece said very little at the time, rather confirming the impression her aunt had herself formed that there was nothing to cause her to worry greatly. But, after some days had passed, the niece rang her up and said that she had been discussing her case with the head surgeon of the hospital to which she was attached and they both agreed that an operation was imperative. The indications were that the source of the bleeding must be healed or the diseased part removed; otherwise there would be difficulty ahead, for the symptoms pointed to malignant disease. The patient asked whether the condition might not clear up of itself. The reply was: 'It is impossible; only surgery will correct it. It will mean three weeks in the hospital and an indefinite period on your second floor, as the use of stairs will not be permissible for you.'

This reply naturally disturbed the lady. Both her husband and an older sister, who in her youth had been like a mother to her, had recently died rather suddenly and she did not feel like facing an operation. Now it chanced that she had heard some time before of an Episcopal Church in the city where Healing Services were held. Remembering this, she made inquiries about it and felt moved to present herself there for healing. This she did on a Thursday morning in the month of September. The rector preached a short sermon and, as he made one point after another, she thought it fitted her exactly and that she could meet every point. At the rector's invitation to those present, removing her hat, she went forward with others and knelt at the altar. She then silently prayed: 'Lord Jesus, You have always kept Your word. You have never broken a promise, and You have said "If hands are laid on and prayer offered, I will heal", so I am depending upon You to do just that.' When the rector's hand was laid upon her head, she says that she experienced a ray of heat going down her body from head to foot. Although she did not understand this at the time, having never heard of such a thing before, she realized at once that she was healed and, as she rose to her feet, she said within herself: 'Thank you, Father, for healing me.'

Towards the end of the month she rang up the physician who had advised an operation and reported that all the symptoms of her haemorrhage had disappeared. His reply was: 'Oh! stopped of themselves, did they?' He asked no further question but, to a relative of hers, he remarked: 'I have a suspicion that my patient has been to ... Church but I should be much more easy in my mind if she were to go to a hospital for a check-up.' She did not go to a hospital; she went instead, in order to satisfy her relatives, to a lady doctor, a specialist of considerable distinction in malignant diseases. After a thorough examination, the specialist said: 'I can find nothing in the world the matter with you; but, if that bleeding starts again, come back to me immediately.' The lady who had been healed replied: 'The bleeding will not start again. God doesn't do things that way.' Writing to me towards the end of April 1953, four and a half years after the healing, she was able to confirm that there had been no return of the haemorrhage.

43 *Melanotic Sarcoma*

The following particulars were obtained from a medical practitioner. They relate to a case observed during the years 1942–4. The patient, a man over 70, was sent to hospital by his doctor and a black tumour of a foot was widely excized by a good surgeon. A section was examined and showed melanotic sarcoma. The area removed was so big that a skin graft was needed. In a short time other tumours appeared and the patient went downhill so fast that, when the doctor went into the Forces, he said to his wife — who was also a doctor and who was left to look after his practice — that he did not expect the man to live more than a few months at most.

At one time seventy blackish swellings were counted on the trunk, the skin nodules averaging the size of a sixpenny piece. There were X-ray evidences of lesions in the tibiae, skull and lungs; the liver was enlarged and the abdomen distended. The patient grew so weak that he could not walk; but he was a very determined man and he would fall out of bed, more or less, crawl along the floor, and pull himself up to the wall to see the world from his window.

When he realized that no more medical aid was forthcoming, he got in touch with some religious friends — thought by the doctor to be Four-square Gospellers — and prayer meetings were held. After this his condition improved. The liver was no longer palpable and X-ray examination showed that the shadows attributable to neoplasms were no longer visible.

The doctor who sent me this report was asked in 1944 to see the man's wife in consultation when she had a severe respiratory infection, and at that time the husband was very active and apparently well. However, he was not equal to nursing his wife, and she was put in a nursing home. The husband caught the infection, rapidly became comatose, and died of a respiratory disease. At post-mortem there were a few fibrous nodes in the mesenteric glands containing pigmented cells regarded as melanomatous, and scars in liver, lungs, and brain. The slides and sections made in 1942 were still available at this date, 1951. The doctor who reported the case and who, so far as I am aware, had no special interest in spiritual healing, expressed the view that it would certainly have been certified as beyond the possibility of cure by medical means.

44 *Carcinoma*

In July 1944 Mrs Saunders, an American, underwent an operation for the radical removal of the left breast. Laboratory tests definitely revealed carcinomatous growths. The surgeon told her that it was a very extensive growth, with nodes all through the chest area, under arm and a small part of the back. He added that if there was a recurrence on that side it would have to be in the bone, because he had removed everything he could possibly remove (muscles, glands, etc.) right down to the bone.

In April 1951 a small lump developed in the left chest area, close to the under-arm section. At about the same time swallowing became difficult occasionally; even drinking water would cause choking; also a cough had been troublesome over a long period. While trying to decide just what to do, the patient awoke one morning to find her voice gone.

She consulted Dr M, who immediately decided to perform a biopsy. The small lump was removed and sent to the laboratory, and on examination carcinoma was again confirmed. The patient was then sent to a throat specialist who diagnosed the loss of voice as due to paralysis of the left vocal chord. The only treatment either doctor could recommend was a course of deep X-ray therapy. After about ten treatments pain developed in the lower ribs, left and right side, and she was sent back to Dr M for further examination and consultation.

By now it was becoming plain to Mrs Saunders that the doctors held out slight hope for her, so she asked

Dr M just what her chances were. He was reluctant to answer but, when she explained that she had a son and she wished to make arrangements for his proper care, he told her that the disease was spreading all through her ribs and chest, and usually in such cases it was 'quite hopeless and quite rapid'. She was to plan for about four months but it might take much longer.

Very conscious of her short-comings, having neglected any close contact with God since childhood and wanting to make her peace with Him, she went to see a minister of the Episcopal Church. He gave her a copy of Dr Rebecca Beard's book, *Everyman's Search*,[7] to read and invited her to attend a Prayer Group on the following Thursday. That book put new hope into her and she finished it before the Thursday. The leader of the Prayer Group then told her of other books to read and made her feel that 'everything would work out all right'.

Writing to me a year later she said that she felt sure she would not still be alive had it not been for the sign-post in *Everyman's Search* showing her the way. Looking back, she recalled that the difficulty she had in swallowing, the cough, and the pain in the ribs seemed all to disappear quite suddenly, though she occasionally still felt a slight discomfort in the area of the ribs. It took quite a while for her voice to return and it was not yet her normal voice, though it sounded quite a natural voice to those who had not known her before. She summed up by saying: 'I feel that my spiritual healing was immediate. The body is sometimes slow in healing, but I know that it still is healing and there is very little evidence of anything out of the ordinary remaining.'

[7] See footnote on p. 19.

As this was a case where, in medical opinion, a recurrence of the original trouble might be feared, even after a longish period of quiescence, I wrote later to ask for a further report from Mrs Saunders. Her reply came on 15 January 1954, in which she states that she has remained perfectly well since she last wrote and has been living a very normal life from day to day, able to do all her own work, including caring for her husband and son, her home and garden. She has reported to her doctor at fairly regular intervals at the doctor's request. Numerous X-ray slides and tests have been made, as if always they 'seem to be expecting to find something', but all reports have been negative. Her voice is still a little husky, and will probably remain so, but does not sound unnatural.

45   *Carcinoma of the Uterus*

The following case is of interest in that the clergyman concerned in it says that he does not claim any gift of healing at all. What he does is 'to try to realize the presence of the risen Christ and to take the sick person into that presence'. He first became aware of the possibilities when, eight years ago, he was called to a hospital to baptize a dying baby. Being deeply moved with compassion he did spontaneously what he now does deliberately and the child immediately recovered.[8] A few days later, he states, he prayed with a little girl of seven, blind after meningitis, and her sight was restored. In his experience, especially with adults, healing usually takes longer. In fact he suspects that 'some patients do not really want to be healed: some older people enjoy the fuss made of them; others make a

[8] He gave as reference to his method, Weatherhead: *Psychology, Religion and Healing*, Section 3, Chs. 1 and 7.

hobby of their illness'. He added that he had not been of much help when trying to heal 'to order'. He thinks there must be real compassion and also, on someone's part, faith.

The case into which I inquired was that of a woman, now about 60, who had had an exploratory operation in 1939. The diagnosis was inoperable carcinoma of the uterus with secondary growths. She was pronounced incurable and this was confirmed by specialists in a more modern hospital to which she was sent when her condition became acute. Her husband was told that she would never leave her bed. This was the position when the clergyman began to visit her. He saw the hospital diagnosis and her own doctor expressed to him the opinion that she would die in a few weeks.

The clergyman's usual practice was to intercede for the patient after administering Holy Communion. He was deeply impressed by her faith. Gradually she began to recover; swellings that had been visible disappeared and in a few days she was up and about. Now, September 1954, after eighteen months, the secondary growths have entirely gone; also the main carcinoma has ceased to be apparent to the patient: it no longer causes pain or inconvenience. She has resumed normal life and incidentally nursed her husband through a serious illness. During this period she developed high blood-pressure and she has had pneumonia and has recovered from both.

46 *Cancer*

A little girl, when she was six months old, was discovered to be the victim of a rare form of cancer which attacked her between the ear and throat. Details of the case were sent to me by a lady who saw the baby when she was making a house-to-house collection for the Cancer Research Fund. The mother said she would willingly contribute, as her child had an incurable cancer. This was eighteen months ago, September 1952, when the child was three and a half years old and 'like a tiny corpse — no life or energy'.

The lady caller was so shocked at her appearance, in fact, that she not only herself 'felt compelled to ask God's help for her recovery' but she also wrote to ask help of the Mr Y of some of our previous cases. In addition many friends of this lady joined at her request in prayers for the child.

The child had had operations and deep radium treatment, but the parents were told that her life had been prolonged only for a short time. After prayers had been offered, however, betterment in health was obvious in a matter of weeks. The child was being taken each month to a London hospital for examination but, in less than six months, the intervals between visits were extended to three months, the specialists reporting their satisfaction and delight that she was so much better.

That little girl is now five years old, and 'full of life, happiness and mischief, in fact, a normal healthy child.' There has been no recurrence of the trouble and, on the last visit to London, the specialist said they 'were amazed at the difference in her and she was very well'. So far the doctors have not been told that 'the child is in the care of God and another healer'.

Visits to the hospital will be continued for a time, although the lady who sent me the particulars of the case expressed the opinion that the child could not look so well and be so energetic if the disease were still active. In his last letter to her Mr Y also trusts that progress will continue from day to day, adding 'so let us give our thanks to God for all His goodness', thereby confirming the impression I had formed that he relies on the same source as more orthodox healers for inspiration in his work.[9]

47 Goitre and High Blood Pressure

An American lady, about fifty years of age, had been suffering for eighteen months or more from an exophthalmic goitre and intense hypertension, her blood-pressure running consistently around 240 to 260. The doctor in charge of the case suggested that she should enter hospital to see what was causing her condition. There various methods were tried to bring the blood-pressure down but they proved ineffective. Finally an operation was proposed for the goitre. To this, however, the patient demurred and, following her sister's advice, she decided instead to go to see a man and wife who together were engaged in spiritual therapy, the wife being medically qualified.[10]

She was exceedingly nervous when she started off on the streetcar. The doctor's wife states that, on arrival, she was 'reeling like a drunken person, with blinding headache and her blood-pressure extremely high'. She told her story and the wife said, 'Well, I think, we'd better get to work' and, while she prayed, the husband laid his hands on the patient, who immediately felt as if the pressure were reduced. To her intense relief her whole body was quieted and, on her return home, she had a good night's rest.

The next day she went by appointment, as was her

[9] See the comments on Mr Y at the end of Case 22.

[10] See previous reference on p. 19 to *Everyman's Search*, by the late Rebecca Beard, which gives a short account of this case (pp. 62, 63). She and Wallace Beard were the spiritual healers concerned in it.

custom, to a high-blood-pressure specialist for a test.
When he had taken her pressure, he rearranged the
machine and repeated the measurement. To his astonishment it again registered only 170, 70 points lower
than he had ever seen it, and he was not satisfied until
he had confirmed the reading on another blood-pressure
gauge.

This occurred in November 1946. The patient was
having no special treatment except that she was taking
pheno-barbitol under the doctor's orders and was on a
salt-free diet. She herself said that she felt as if the drop
in her blood pressure could have lasted had she 'stayed
on the beam'; but the first time she lost her temper, and
she acknowledges that she had a hot one, up went the
blood-pressure. She found that it took some time before
nothing disturbed her and she could remain calm and
composed, turning to God for help in giving up old
habits. In fact at the beginning of 1947 she went to stay
with Wallace and Rebecca Beard for three months and
underwent a course of daily meditation with the aid of
their ministry and gradually, according to Dr Beard,
'her goitre disappeared and her high blood-pressure
became a thing of the past'.

In August, 1954, she informed me that, if she has
occasion now to see another doctor as a friend, and he
wishes to take her blood-pressure, she allows it. Usually
the count is normal; occasionally it may be a little high
according to the emotional quality of her living at the
time, but she always ignores it and refuses to allow
anything to fill her with fear again.

48 *Handicapped Children*

A university qualified social worker, Miss Taylor, of

some experience in successful pioneering work of different kinds, undertook the direction of a pilot experiment with a small group of mentally defective children suffering from additional handicaps. There were in all twelve children, seven boys and five girls, ranging from $6\frac{1}{2}$ to 15 years of age and with intelligence quotients from 31 to 87. They were selected by the medical officer and staff psychologist out of the large number admitted to a hospital for mentally deficient children. Six of them had been grossly deaf, from birth or a very early age, and had consequently never learnt to speak; two more were afflicted with considerable deafness, one being also dumb and the other having only very defective speech. Of the remaining four: one could hear slightly and was able to repeat isolated words; another had almost normal hearing but suffered from a curious form of aphasia, missing out all consonants in speaking; and although the other two could hear quite well, one of them could speak but little, and that poorly, while the second had only limited speech and no use of the legs, both children being afflicted with cerebral palsy — as were two of the six described above as grossly deaf. The cerebral trouble resulted in grave inco-ordination in one of the two latter children and in little rapport in the other.

Children suffering from serious mental defect may not be educable, even in a special school, and the purpose of this pilot experiment was to discover whether it was largely on account of their additional handicap, their deafness or their inability to speak properly, that any of these children perhaps appeared to be more lacking in intelligence than they really were. If they could be taught to hear and speak, even moderately well, and if they were then given another intelligence test, it was just possible that one or more of them might be rated high enough to attend a special school.

With that possibility in view, Miss Taylor arranged to give them tuition on three afternoons a week for a period of three months. If the experiment proved successful, the intention was to appoint a full-time teacher to continue the instruction on an expanded scale.

Now it so happened that Miss Taylor was in touch with a Prayer Group of Christian people interested in spiritual healing, as she herself was, and she told them of this experiment and asked if they would remember her twelve children in their weekly prayers. This they promised to do and one of them, along with Miss Taylor, agreed to pray each day for the children, not only as a group but each having also one individual child in mind every day.

The twelve children had previously occupied different wards for sleeping and for meals in the hospital and they had attended different classes in the occupation centre. Now for the first time they were brought into touch with each other and it was surprising to see how soon, in view of their similar handicaps, they began to enjoy one another's company. What was even more remarkable was the spontaneous effort they made to help one another; those who could hear tried hard to help the deaf to understand what was said to them and the deaf tried to help those who could not walk. This further comment was added by their teacher: 'They are extremely patient with the one who has gross inco-ordination, and in games requiring finger manipulation — which is difficult for him — they never attempt to play out of turn or to leave him out.'

The general conclusion at the end of the course was that four children showed marked improvement in speech and understanding, and with two of these very little contact had been made before. All four could give and carry out simple instructions, act simple stories read to them by their teacher, and describe in short sentences the pictures in their books. They learnt to count up to ten, and they could match words with pictures on fifteen cards. The names of all the children were written out on different cards and they could recognize the different names and give the cards to the right children. Five others in the twelve made some progress but it was not so striking, while the remaining three showed no improvement at all. Lack of progress in these three was evidently due to mental disability rather than deafness, although even they evinced more interest than before in what was going on around them.

The Deputy Medical Superintendent of the hospital was amazed at the improvement in the children and he considered that the experiment had fully justified itself. He asked if he might invite the Chairman of the Governing Body to come and see the class, and eventually he and other members came. A little demonstration and play were staged to show what the children could do and it went off surprisingly well.

It is, of course, impossible to say how much of this success was due to the patience and ability of the teacher and how much to the prayers offered on behalf of the children. It would not be unreasonable perhaps to assume that both made some contribution towards it.

49 *Mongoloid Children*

I now return to Miss Heaton, the subject of Case 24. For some years now she has been ministering to mongoloid children. That came about in this way: while helping to nurse a sick friend and her mother, she was praying one day and asking God what next, when a picture of a child's face appeared on the wall, then another, and another. She says that all the children whose pictures were seen then have since been under her care. She had previously helped a patient of the man who had ministered to her own healing who was a member of the Church of England, and the vicar had observed this lady getting well through her ministration. He preached, shortly after, a sermon on healing when he mentioned that one in his parish was obeying Christ's command to heal the sick. In the congregation was a mother with a mongoloid child. Medical specialists and many less orthodox healers had been consulted about the child without avail, and now the mother just held on to the hope that God would yet answer her prayers. After the service she made inquiries for Miss Heaton's address. The next day she and a child of 11 were on her doorstep.

The outcome of that inquiry was that Miss Heaton went to live with the parents of the child and helped to train her and other children. She remained with them for several years and she told me that she had never wanted for anything. About a year ago she needed a gramophone and records for her children. She made it a matter of prayer and, before nine o'clock that same night, they were in her hands as gifts for use in God's work.

Quite recently the way has opened in a remarkable manner for the expansion of her work with backward children. A fine commodious house in the west country has been bought for this purpose and a capable staff has been provided which she is to direct. To quote again a previous remark she made: 'What you attend to and concentrate upon enters your life'; that is the principle upon which she bases her work. She says she is never interested in what people have wrong with them, and she will never let them talk about it or fill their minds with a picture of disharmony. She begins straightway to bring them into Christ's presence and seeks to hold them there until they themselves look above the body to Him.

One example will suffice to illustrate the almost incredible results which Miss Heaton has achieved with these subnormal children. Molly came to her at the age of twelve. She could neither read nor write a two-lettered word and she did not seem to know her own name. I have seen photographs of her at different stages of her development. When first seen her mouth was open, the tongue being very evident and the eyes nearly closed. A month later the eyes were opened, the tongue was not noticeable, and she had begun to speak and learn her alphabet. After six months she showed a real interest in everything. She went forward steadily, learning to read, write and knit; also she was speaking much more clearly. In a year she was getting to be quite a nice looking girl. The last photograph shows Molly on her confirmation day, a candidate with over eighty others.

That child was with Miss Heaton for three years. When she went back to her mother she proved to be quite a help in the home. She was able to read her Bible; she could sing, knit, sew and do many of the things girls of her age should do. She had become, in fact, a beautiful child who promised to be a great joy to her family.

This sequel to Miss Heaton's own healing story is one of the most remarkable in my series, because it concerns a region of the mind which is generally regarded as beyond hope of any striking improvement. It may fittingly be concluded with a doctor's testimony. He writes as follows:

The wonder of the human race is that so many of us are born normal. Some are incomplete in mind and body, but in them a spiritual being can be born. Miss Heaton has proved this beyond doubt as witnessed in the miracles of children she has cared for. She has proved that, with insistence on the development of the Spirit in communion with the Eternal in the simple ways that Christ taught, these unfortunate children will gradually grow to understand the realities of life and develop a spiritual awareness.

Their physical state and reactions improve, also their appearance and mental acuity. And this in spite of the well-known fact of their brain substance being very much diminished. Now, instead of their weak bodies controlling their minds, they develop a Spiritual being which takes control of the mind and, through the mind, control of the body.

It is quite an experience to see these developed children taking responsibility for each other, their appearance, physical attitude and occupations. This is pioneer work indeed!

Part Three

INDIAN RECORDS

I have placed the rest of my healing cases here for two reasons: they all come from India and for information about them I am entirely dependent upon records kept by Bishop Q and Col R, respectively, who ministered to their healing. Also, because of the lapse of time since healing occurred, it would have been impossible to trace many of the patients themselves had I attempted to follow them up; consequently the particulars available are not as full as those relating to cases included in Part II.

Readers should refer back at this point to my note introducing Case 25 in Part II, where I explain how I first made contact with Bishop Q and Col R. I start here with half a dozen cases sent to me by Col R who, it will be recalled, is an experienced medical doctor. In addition to his professional work at college, he was in charge of a Cathedral alms-house from which some of his patients came.

Col R's Records

No. 1. Miss Arnold was under his observation in 1932, when she had been suffering about six months. She was a Eurasian, aged about 54, living in the alms-house. Col R's diagnosis was cancer of the cervix of the uterus with extensive secondaries. This was confirmed by the Professor of Gynaecology who judged it to be too far gone for operative treatment.

The patient was a convinced believer in the healing power of Christ and she herself, Col R, the Deaconess, and the Matron and inmates of the alms-house all engaged in prayer on her behalf. Recovery began immediately; the pain and the appalling smell went quite quickly but it took about three months for all trace of the cancer to disappear. The patient was having no medical treatment at the time which could account for this healing and there was no recurrence of any of the symptoms of the disease. The cure was complete and it lasted until the woman died eight years later from pneumonia.

No. 2. Mrs Bunch was an old lady of 80, also Eurasian and living in the alms-house. She had been troubled for two months with severe neuritis, which began soon after and in all likelihood as the result of a badly set Colles fracture. As soon as prayer had been offered by the patient and Col R, the pain left her and never returned. This happened ten years ago and she was under no medical treatment which might conceivably have contributed to the cure.

No. 3. An Indian lad was brought to Col R, in 1949, who had been suffering for about a week from pyelitis with retention of urine which had caused paralysis of both legs. A Kahn test was negative and catheterisation produced no improvement.

Col R and a medical colleague interested in the case asked the Deanery Chairman if he would be good enough to hold a Service of Healing and lay hands on the sick lad. This was done and two hours after the service the patient passed urine without assistance. On the next day he began to move his legs a little, and four days later he walked out of the hospital unaided. He did not return — as he most likely would have done, had it been necessary, in view of the benefit he had previously received — so the presumption is that he was cured permanently.

The doctor remarked that the medical treatment he was receiving might have helped him to get better, but the speed of healing seemed to be greater than could be attributed to drugs alone.

No. 4. In contrast with this last case my informant mentioned that a child, two and a half years old, was present at the same Healing Service. She had tuberculous bronchial glands resulting in miliary tuberculosis of both lungs. In her case no improvement was manifest and she died. I asked the doctor if he had any comment to make on this, and he replied by quoting Bishop Q who had had long experience of divine healing: 'Healing is not granted in such cases because God has some better gift to bestow. We see things piece-meal in time, whereas He sees the matter whole in eternity. Thus we are not in a position to make a proper judgment. For instance, to adults the gift of holiness may be given, enabling them to bear an important witness.'

The doctor himself added:

Another possible aspect of failure to heal is the type of prayer made. To think of the patient as sick when you pray for healing is not the prayer of faith. 'What things soever ye desire, when ye pray, believe that ye have them and they will be given.' A relation or friend may hinder the healing if his attention is concentrated on disease. . . . I expect you remember how Ambrose Pare, surgeon to the French king in about the thirteenth century, used to say 'I treated him, but God cured him'. This is the true state of affairs. The more scientific medicine has become, the more materialistic it has become. We regard penicillin, etc., as cures. We forget the divine part, healing. Man only treats. We have a tendency to run to God for help when we are in a fix and don't know what to do. We should acknowledge His healing power in the simplest injury or disease. Health is as great a marvel as healing, when you consider the intricate processes going on in the body; for instance, the percentage of glucose (sugar) in normal blood which is maintained within very narrow maximum and minimum limits. . . . It seems to me that a long life, especially a healthy life in the bodily sense, imposes a responsibility on old people. They cannot claim that they have not had a chance. Few people remember to give thanks for health; they take it as a matter of course.[1]

No. 5. The following case was reported by Dr B, a colleague of Col R. It was observed at another hospital which he visited professionally. It relates to a Hindu youth who came to the hospital in 1948 with a fracture of the spine resulting in paralysis of both legs. This had occurred about twelve months prior to his attendance at the hospital. The youth and his family were preparing for baptism; and he wished to serve the Church after training as a teacher.

The Manager of a Church Settlement ministered to the patient at two Healing Services. An improvement in his condition took place after the first Service, but it was slow; it became more rapid after the second. In about two months he was able to walk but not run. It is believed that the cure was lasting, for there has been no news of any relapse. The patient was having no medical treatment which could account for the recovery.

No. 6. This was a young woman with tuberculosis, attending the hospital as an out-patient. The symptoms were fever, loss of appetite and weight, pain, and large

[1] The remarkable adaptability of the processes going on ceaselessly within the human body is brought out very clearly by Dr Alexis Carrel, to whom previous reference has been made (p. 13). See his *Man, the Unknown* and *Reflections on Life* (Hamish Hamilton, 1952).

hard masses of glands in the abdomen. She had been suffering for six months or longer before coming to hospital.

The patient's mother was told that medical treatment would probably not be successful; she must pray. Being a Hindu, she asked: 'Can I pray to my God?' She was answered in the affirmative and shown a written prayer. The patient and her mother then attended prayers in the out-patient department of the hospital.

The response was surprisingly quick. After continued attendance for six weeks at the hospital, the last report from the doctor, 2 September 1953, stated that there was no fever; the glands in the abdomen were then only palpable with care, and the patient was putting on weight. She was still receiving medical attention, taking nicolabine tablets, shark oil, A.P.C. tablets, and extra milk. Her family were too poor to afford streptomycin. This is a case where the doctor's treatment and his manner of dealing with the patient no doubt made a significant contribution to the cure.

Bishop Q's Records

I now pass on to particulars of cases recorded by Bishop Q. He was good enough to send me notes which he had compiled over a period of more than forty years on some of the very large number of cases which had passed through his hands in the course of his ministry. I was particularly struck by the methodical way in which these notes were recorded, giving in few words just the essential and significant facts about each case, and faithfully including the failures as well as the successes so far as their physical healing was concerned.

The bishop is an Irishman, who has spent most of his life in India. As a priest, he began anointing for healing, with his bishop's permission, and continued this ministry after himself becoming a bishop. He had some success in healing before he began anointing, but the cures were infrequent. All the records sent to me relate to patients who had been anointed. The bishop does not claim to have any special gift; he rests simply on Christ's command and promises to the Church. To quote from one of his letters to me, in response to a request for information as to the precise procedure adopted by him: 'I carefully prepare the patient in soul and mind, deal faithfully with sin, and lead to repentance; call for faith and self-surrender; bid the sick person seek first the glory of Christ, whether in healing or in some other way, and then come another day with others for the service of anointing, taken in my canonicals, according to a form I have drawn up from various sources.'

His records start from 1912, and he sent me a statistical analysis of his observations on all cases up to 1919. This record was very carefully prepared for a Committee appointed by Canadian Bishops to investigate the subject of divine healing. It is to be regretted that he never saw a report by them, if indeed one was ever published. In the table which follows I have rearranged his figures and, omitting the forty-two cases, 12 per cent of the total, on which no medical report was obtained, I have calculated percentages to show what happened to the rest of the patients. It will be seen that the failures amounted to 27.7 per cent of the total and that there was some measure of success, partial if not complete, in all the rest, 72.3 per cent of the total. Those who fully recovered numbered nearly one-third of all reported upon and, if we include those who showed a marked improvement, the proportion was

54 per cent. Only 7·1 per cent. had a relapse. The bishop told me that he had consistently noticed that a great spiritual blessing is nearly always experienced from this ministry, whether healing follows or not.[2] Only in exceptional cases is it his practice to anoint a person more than once for the same sickness. Often considerable numbers come on two successive days for teaching and instruction, followed on the third day by anointing.

ANALYSIS OF PATIENTS ANOINTED BY BISHOP Q
(April 1912 to June 1919)

Total number of patients anointed	353	
No medical report on . .	42	11·9 per cent.
Number of patients reported on	311	100·0 per cent.
Fully recovered . . .	100	32·1 per cent.
Marked improvement . .	68	21·9 ,, ,,
Some improvement . . .	35	11·2 ,, ,,
Recovery and relapse . .	11 ⎫	
Improvement and relapse .	11 ⎬ 7·1 ,, ,,	
No improvement . . .	48 ⎫	
Died	38 ⎭ 27·7 ,, ,,	

[2] This is of particular interest in view of the fact that opinion is divided — even among those who have a profound belief in the value of spiritual healing — as to the wisdom of practising it in large gatherings open to the general public. The fear is expressed that it may result in loss of faith on the part of any patients who may be bitterly disappointed if, after prayer and the laying on of hands, they remain unhealed. On the other side it is claimed that, while this may happen in exceptional cases, the more general experience is that even those who are not healed share in a revival of the spirit, which cannot but be beneficial to their bodily condition also. Attention is frequently drawn to this fact in the story of J. M. Hickson's World Healing Mission. It will be noted that Bishop Q was careful to prepare his patients before the public session. That is no doubt very desirable whenever possible.

I am sure, judging from his letters, that the bishop would be the first to admit that, where there was any measure of success, the skill of the doctors and the care of the nurses — under divine guidance — frequently contributed to it. But, no less frequently, if we may judge by his notes, stress is laid on the powerful influence of divine healing at work in the patient at the same time.

All his patients, whether English, Eurasian, or Indian, were said to belong to a more or less cultured and educated class[3]. The great majority were either very bad, chronic, or desperate cases with but slight hope of recovery. Nearly all the doctors in control were Hindu; not infrequently either there was no diagnosis or it was not highly skilled.

The following are, in the words of the bishop, examples of 'severe cases of organic disease healed through the Ministry of Prayer, where the diagnosis was good presumably, and where the recovery does not seem to have been due to medical treatment, or only partly so'. They relate to the period 1912 to 1936. I have picked out fifteen records only from his long list, as samples of the brief notes kept by the bishop about his patients, using the following abbreviations for the sex and nationality of each:

M male, F female; E English, Eu Eurasian, I Indian. Also, the patient's age, when known, is inserted after these letters.

---

[3] The terms 'cultured' and 'educated' are no doubt to be understood as relative terms in an Indian setting. In reading Hickson's *Heal the Sick* (see p. 5) the impression is certainly given that 'the charismatic gift operates more effectively upon simple, childlike natures than upon the more complex, highly civilized persons' (p. 135), and that is what one might expect.

1. F, E 71. Abcess and erysipelas of face. Doctors in consultation very doubtful of recovery. Day after anointing temperature normal, well in eleven days.

2. F, Eu 30. Four months in three hospitals with tubercular enteritis and chronic diarrhoea. Last doctor wrote: 'I did not think there was any chance of her recovery.' Anointed three times, the third time when she was said to be dying. Complete recovery.

3. F, E. Incipient phthisis both lungs. Some pericarditis and bad attacks of cardiac dropsy. In bed five months. Improvement began day after anointing; in a few weeks able to be up; in seven months able to take up maternity nursing and continues working despite occasional heart attacks.

4. F, I 8. Hereditary syphilis. Wasserman test positive, diagnosis of specialist. Dr reported very little hope of recovery. Girl wasting away for four and a half years. After anointing, perfectly well in three weeks. Same specialist tested blood and result negative. Reports of the child received for three years subsequently stated that she remained quite well.

5. F, E 20. Left eye diseased since infancy. Operation at age of six followed by eight others to age of 19. Sightless except for seeing a luminous circle for twelve months. Specialist pronounced case hopeless and recommended glass eye. Next day after anointing reported ability to see clock. Second day, skin dropped from eye and she saw clearly. A few weeks later skin again dropped and sight further improved. Report three years later, eye quite right; never wears glasses and can see quite well.

6. F, E. Jaundice. Most rapid recovery after anointing. Dr in charge said: 'I have never seen jaundice clear away so rapidly.'

7. M, Eu 21. Leprosy[4] four years; student in medical college. Healing began immediately after anointing. Took up work as doctor in leper asylum, progressed steadily in health and strength. Reported himself as quite well six years later. Worked for many years as a leper doctor and the medical verdict was that, though the disease was still there, it was inactive and non-infectious. Allowed to live where he liked.

8. M, I 20. Phthisis right lung. Very bad case. Sanatorium for nine months previously without improvement. After anointing steady improvement. Two-and-a-half years after, lungs examined and pronounced quite free.

9. F, Eu 19. In general hospital with heart disease considered incurable. Steady improvement from day of anointing; in twenty-eight days discharged cured. Reports for four years show no relapse.

10 F, Eu 65. One doctor diagnosed enteric and felt growth in womb which he diagnosed as cancer. Another doctor confirmed cancer but not enteric. Both said operation useless and patient could not live more than a month. Rapid and complete recovery after anointing; walked unaided to church fourteen days after to return thanks and lived for many years.

11. M, E 14, Tubercular peritonitis two years. Operations had been performed for appendicitis and adhesions but unsuccessful. Bowels exuding from side caused intense discomfort. Local doctor considered case hopeless and specialist unwilling to operate again. After anointing, steady improvement. Had reports for a year, when the boy was able to go to school nearly well.

12. F, Burmese 31. Rheumatism right knee one-and-

---

[4] This case came under observation before the date of the discovery of new methods for curing leprosy.

a-half years, swells if she walks, unable to walk quarter mile. Healed instantaneously at anointing and able to walk eight to ten miles easily seven months later.

13. M, I 43. Congestion of liver for one year. Stiffness of hip joints for two months, unable to stand. Gained power to stand immediately after anointing. Improvement in walking was gradual and finally complete. In six months the liver was perfectly all right. In touch for many years and no return.

14. F, E 60. Cataract and angina pectoris. A month after the anointing reported: 'The cataract cleared away entirely to the amazement of the specialist.' Eyesight has continued perfect and the heart, despite some bad attacks, has not prevented her living a very active life. In touch with this case up to 1939.

15. F, E ?50. Glaucoma, recently operated. Two specialists told her not to expect ever to see much with that eye; but the day after the anointing it cleared up wonderfully, and sixteen months later she was seeing better without glasses than previously with them.

I add five more recent cases with assumed names, which I have abstracted from a list compiled by the bishop in 1942–8.

Dr Charles, aged 56, was suffering from neuritis and dermatitis of the right arm and was unable to lift it. She had had medical treatment but was no better when she came to the bishop for anointing on 11 September 1942. She reported to him just a month later that the neuritis was almost cured but not the dermatitis. By 29 November the neuritis was stated to be quite healed and a later report, 7 December, confirmed that she remained free of the neuritis. She thought that the continuance of the dermatitis was due to grievous family trouble.

Mrs Dawson came to see the bishop, a heavy weight having fallen on her leg twenty years before, in 1920, causing a very painful lymphangitis if she walked. It improved with medical attention but the doctors said that no more treatment would be of any use. She last reported to the bishop six months after her anointing in 1942. The leg had by then much improved and there was very little swelling, although she had been obliged to be on her feet a good deal on account of an operation to her husband followed by a long illness.

Mrs Ellis, aged about 40 in June 1948, had been married twelve years, and each time when a baby was expected she got fits and there was no birth.[5] A baby was expected in November 1948, and the prospective mother was greatly relieved because, after anointing, she had freedom from fits and her baby was born.

Stephen French, a young man just under 30, began in 1942 with a very bad attack of polyneuritis. The bishop prayed for him from June of that year and, during that time, he made some progress. In May, 1944, he had a bad relapse, but he got very much better immediately after anointing. Subsequent reports up to February 1946 point to steady but slow progress.

Geraldine, a child of twelve, got aphasia on 11 November 1942, after a long illness. The bishop prayed for her from that time but there was no speech, although in all other respects she was a clever and intelligent child and was continuing with her studies. On 4 January 1948, speech returned, at first only a few words, becoming soon entirely normal. The bishop kept in touch with her until 11 April 1948.

[5] Presumably a miscarriage resulted.

Part Four

A DOCTOR'S COMMENT

By J. BURNETT RAE, M.B., CH.B.

Hon. Consulting Physician to Croydon General Hospital, and Vice-Chairman of the Churches' Council of Healing.

In view of the fact that disease, or the risk of it in one form or another, is never far from any one of us and that many have an almost morbid interest in it, or dread of it, this book should have a wide appeal. There are some for whom it may well mean even more than this; for them it may seem to open up a vista of renewed hope in health and life.

Canon Raven has drawn attention in his foreword to the author's qualifications for the work he has essayed, to his suitability for relating and evaluating the interesting facts he has collected: these the author has presented in a form well calculated to indicate their significance.

As I have not had the opportunity of dealing with any of the cases recorded, my comments must necessarily be of a general character, but I welcome the chance of saying something on the important subject of Spiritual Healing in connection with those cases which, taken as a whole, are most impressive and lead one to some definite conclusions.

Before stating these I would like to say that any doctor would approve the restraint with which Mr Caradog Jones — not himself a doctor — has presented his material. One is favourably impressed by the fact that he does not claim too much, and that throughout he insists that spiritual healing is not an alternative to medical and more ordinary methods of treatment, but should always seek to be associated with them, supplementing and augmenting their efficiency.

Our author is well aware of the difficulties, both theological and medical involved in the subject, pointing out in his Introduction, for example, that 'if some cures occur with little or no faith on the part of the patient, it might be expected that anyone with much faith would certainly be cured. The truth, however, is that, even given a large measure of faith on the part of the patient, healing is by no means assured', and also that 'the impression gained by a close study of the subject is that the proportion of persons permanently cured by spiritual healing is not high.'

I have no intention of tackling the theological problems for my concern is with the medical implications of the subject as our author has presented it, but even so one finds it is virtually impossible to keep the theological and the medical aspects of the matter entirely apart for it is the relationship of the two which is precisely what one is dealing with all the time. My hope is that what I say may have a practical bearing on a most interesting and important matter for us all.

I am asked as a doctor to comment upon the place which this body of evidence may reasonably take in the world of medical science. In view of the immense problems, scientific, moral, and religious, which are involved, this is no easy — indeed it is an almost impossible — task in the space at my disposal. Nor am I much helped by the reflection that I approach the matter from the specialist viewpoint of a psychiatrist. It does however help me to begin my survey, because the greatly increased interest in what is called Spiritual Healing has largely come about through the investigations of medical psychologists.

The trail was blazed by physicians such as Elliotson, James Braid, Charcot, Bernheim, Pierre Janet, Milne Bramwell and others who worked out the psychology of hypnotism and suggestion, and demonstrated the influence which states of mind have upon health. Following upon them came Freud, Jung, Adler and others of the analytical school, who investigated the influence of the unconscious in health and disease. We began to hear of complexes, repressed instincts, endo-psychic conflicts, sublimations and other terms now in common use. Also among the pioneers should be mentioned psychologists like William James and William McDougall, whose interest in the subject was mainly philosophic, and who pointed out its relation to social and religious thought.

Theologians and churchmen could not be indifferent to all this. It had become once again obvious that as a man 'thinketh in his heart, so is he'; out of the heart proceed not only the best that a man can think and do, but also evil and disease. They were reminded forcefully of their Lord's commission not only to preach the Gospel but to heal the sick, and became acutely aware that they had delegated an essential part of their business to a profession which in many respects was less fitted to deal with it than themselves. But acceptance of the fact that medical men, by their training and experience, are better able to track down the causes of disease, has produced a desire for mutual study and co-operation.

Our author has mentioned the leading part which

William Temple took in bringing together clergy and doctors to work out the implications of this, but the Archbishop was by no means the first Churchman at work in this field. One should remember also the pioneer labours of Harold Anson, Percy Dearmer, Lily Dougal, H.H.Workman, Malcolm Spencer, as well as those mentioned in the Introduction. A result of all this research and effort is the renewed interest in spiritual healing, and it is very remarkable.

Some thirty years ago the medical profession was invited by the Archbishop of York to consider together with the clergy the interest and concern which both professions have in the prevention and cure of disease. While sympathetic to the invitation, the doctors declined as they felt they might be drawn into considerations outside the scope of their own proper activities. This attitude no longer obtains. The advance of scientific thought, especially along the lines of psychosomatic medicine which concerns itself with the influence of the mental and emotional factors upon both health and disease, has produced a very different outlook. All over the country clergy and doctors are meeting together not only to study and discuss these matters, but also to work out their practical implications. It has become obvious that it is not enough to point out to a patient the influence which fear, anxiety, resentment or jealousy may have upon the functions of his mind or body; these emotions must be controlled or changed. In view of these facts, the Church has begun to waken up to the strength of her position.

In the early days of the Christian Church healings took place very similar to those described by our author. These were expected in view of the fact that Christ had commissioned His Apostles to carry on His healing work as an essential part of His Gospel. Unfortunately credulity and superstition gradually crept in. The line between faith and magic, both in the Church and in medicine, has always been a fine one; the magician and the medicine man, and even the doctor today, have always found it both difficult to define and tempting to ignore. The danger was obviously greater in an unscientific age, when the prevalent view of miracles was one of God not only intervening in the order of nature, but contravening its laws. Medical science as it advanced had to dissociate itself from this, and gradually the division between medicine and religion became definite. This has had its advantages, but it has also in some respects been disastrous. It has created the impression that between the physical and spiritual aspects of man's life there is a great gulf fixed; that they are subject to different laws and have really little to do with each other.

When I was a medical student this was certainly the prevailing attitude. Even devout Christian doctors, agreeing with it, kept their religion in one compartment, and their science in another. It is quite true of course that the spiritual and the physical are very different. Berdyaev, the Russian philosopher, says that the real dualism is not between mind and body but between nature and spirit. That which is born of flesh is flesh, and that which is born of spirit is spirit. They are different, but they are very closely related and necessary to each other.

Let us examine the matter more closely, in the setting provided by the facts which our author presents. We are helped to realize the true relationship of body and spirit when we recognize the distinction between them. We must not fall into the error of confusing things that belong to different planes. To do so cannot make for any reasonable co-operation between men of faith and men of science.

The first difference we might note is that science deals with the general and uniform, whereas religion is concerned with personal and individual affairs. There is a tendency on the part of some to believe that there is something peculiarly spiritual about vibrations, electromagnetic, radionic, and others; that these have some special affinity with the Divine. But when one has resolved matter into molecules, and molecules into atoms and electrons, when matter and energy are shown to be almost one and the same thing, the essential difference between the material and the spiritual still remains. The issue between these must be settled on other grounds than that of the constitution of matter.

We should treat disease as far as possible on its own level, physical, mental, or spiritual, for each is subject to laws which we disregard at our peril. The physical is subject to the laws of chemistry and dynamics, the mind is not. Man has problems which do not beset other creatures, but he also has powers which animals do not possess. The effect of an injury on a person is determined, not simply by the character of the injury, but by the way in which the individual takes it. And that is now the attitude of medical science towards disease. Disease is not just the bodily effect of the germ or the injury, but includes any adverse mental or spiritual reaction to this on the part of the patient.

A patient of mine, when a boy, overheard the doctor telling his mother that he had a weak heart and that she must be exceptionally careful. This well-meant advice coloured the whole of his life. He was always afraid of doing too much, and frightened by the slightest disturbance of the heart's action. He developed what we call a cardiac neurosis.

The doctor, like others, believes in the value of diagnosis, of ascertaining the cause of any disease or disaster. Pain and disease are not meaningless; they are drawing attention to something wrong which we must endeavour to put right. Only when this has been done are we justified in removing the distressing symptom by medical, mental, spiritual or other means. To remove acute abdominal pain before ascertaining and dealing with its cause, would amount to medical malpractice.

If there has been a railway accident we institute an enquiry into it. In this way we prevent its recurrence; it is not enough to pray about it, although prayer may inspire and help the investigation. So it is when dealing with disease. If we could discover the cause of cancer we should be in a much better position to know how it could be cured and prevented. This principle is equally true in the treatment of mental disorders. We must understand the mechanisms at work.

But it is never enough to diagnose. We may know only too well the causes of disease. What we have to do is to bring alongside the painful fact another fact, a greater fact; then out of their interaction a new fact arises. This applies at all levels: it is the Christian as well as the medical method. The doctor applies it when he increases the resistance of his patient by the use of a vaccine or an antidote. In Christian healing St Paul describes it in his statement 'Where sin abounded, grace did much more abound': or again 'The law of the Spirit of life in Christ Jesus hath made me free from the law of sin and death'.

This principle takes us to the heart of our investigation. Our Lord said He came not to destroy the law but to fulfil it. He was no doubt referring to the Mosaic law; but it might apply equally to natural law. Religion does not nullify or disregard this; it brings alongside the laws of nature other laws, higher laws, which alter the situation. There is nothing exceptional about this; we see it constantly operating at all levels of life and between these levels. It accounts for what is called psychosomatic medicine: the influence which the mind has upon the body, and the body upon the mind, both for good and ill. In this connexion we might note that, in the majority of cases with which we have to deal, the disorder is not in the body or in the mind, but in a breakdown of relationship between the two. This accounts for the fact that, among those who come for advice, it is estimated that 30 per cent of all medical out-patients seek it for ailments which are primarily psychoneurotic in origin.

Spiritual healing is of course concerned with all aspects of health and disease, with organic conditions as well as with functional disorders. I refer only to the latter to point out the constant interaction that is going on between the different aspects and levels of human life, for it is this fact which makes spiritual healing not only Christian but scientific.

It can never be merely a useful adjuvant to other forms of healing. It is central in all healing for it springs out of the fact of our nature and destiny. Man, as Berdyaev says, is a strange creature, a profound riddle to himself, bearing witness to the existence of a higher world, but discontented with himself, both base and lofty, weak and strong, free and slavish with his roots in heaven and also in the nethermost depths. Out of this fact comes his problem. Inspired and frightened by his own thoughts, frustrated by his conflicting emotions and desires; living in two worlds, the material and the spiritual, the ways and interests of which appear so often to be conflicting, he is often the victim of tensions affecting his mind and his muscles, his nervous system and all the glands and organs which they control; hence come many of the disorders which we are apt to suppose are purely physical in character, to be cured only by physical or material means.

Dr R.R.Bomford, Physician to the London Hospital, in his Bradshaw Lecture (1952) on Changing Concepts in Health and Disease said 'Strictly there can be no such thing as psychosomatic medicine or psychosomatic disease, for health and disease are necessarily psychosomatic, so there cannot be a part of medicine or some diseases which are psychosomatic. ... It is perfectly true that in some cases much information may be given by physical, and little by psychological methods, and in others much by psychological, and little by physical methods; but we must not be tempted to conclude from this that there are physical diseases and psychological diseases.' He concluded his lecture with words which are very significant: 'The time will come when clinical medicine will be regarded neither as an art nor as a science in itself, but as a special kind of relationship between two persons, a doctor and a patient. It will be recognized that this relationship is the essential feature of clinical medicine; and that the degree of success that it has, depends, as in other human affairs, on the skill with which both science and art are called to its aid.' These words of a distinguished physician are significant because, if true, as I believe them to be, they are applicable not only to the necessary *rapport* between a patient and his doctor, but to that supreme relationship of man with God, the Divine Healer.

The relationship of the patient to the physician is important but there is a more ultimate relationship which determines all others, that of man to God. When this is right all others tend to come right. One sees everything in a different perspective, especially oneself. 'I must abide in God,' said St Augustine, 'for if I abide not in Him, I cannot abide in myself.'

The psychologist has little difficulty in agreeing with Dr Bomford, because for him the *rapport* between the patient and the physician is a sine-qua-non of psychotherapeutic treatment, but it is well that he also mentions the importance of the physician's skill and science. It is obvious that the value of any relationship must depend upon the contribution made by the partners concerned — by the doctor and by the patient. 'If I had appendicitis,' said a clergyman to me, 'I would rather be treated by a skilful pagan than by an incompetent saint': and so say all of us. But if your trouble were of the mind rather than of the body, if you were constantly being frustrated, not so much by circumstances without as by conditions within, so that you were unable to unify the instinctive tendencies of your nature, and could not bring them into line with your duties and ideals, whom under these circumstances would you be wise to consult, the scientific pagan, or the man with an understanding of the human heart and its relationship to the Divine?

This background is of the utmost importance in healing. But the foreground is also important. We are intended to use our own common sense as well as the skill and knowledge of others. God will not do for us what we can and should do for ourselves, but have we not all noticed that sometimes, when we have done everything we can and found it insufficient, man's

extremity becomes God's opportunity; that when without reserve we throw ourselves upon the power and
love of God, something happens. The problem has then
shifted from the purely physical or mental to the
spiritual, and as Maeterlinck says 'it is in the soul that
the great things happen'. The psychological moment
seems to have arrived when something can be done for
us which we could never do for ourselves.

It will be noticed that in one of his early sections, the
author describes cases of functional mental and nervous
disorders. Most doctors, certainly all who have a
Christian outlook, would regard these as suitable for
spiritual therapy if it is wisely and knowledgeably
practised, and in conjunction with any medical treatment that is required.

When we move on in the book to cases of an organic
nature, where physical effects sometimes of a structural
character are present, we may expect less agreement.
There are Christian theologians who think that the
ministry of healing as practised in New Testament times
by Jesus and his Apostles was not intended to continue,
its function being to authenticate the Messiahship of
our Lord, and that it came to a natural end when this
was achieved. To support this view, it has seemed
necessary to draw a hard and fast line between the
healing works recorded in the New Testament and cases
such as doctors and spiritual healers now succeed in
curing. They will accept cases of a purely functional or
mental character but become critical of any claims
which seem to be in line with the cases of cure described
in the Scriptures.

As a psychiatrist I recognize the distinction between
functional and organic cases. It is a useful and necessary
distinction but I do not accept it as fundamental.

Structural disease produces functional disorder, and in time functional disharmony will produce actual structural organic changes. They are very closely related.

We shall go into this in some detail presently. I am concerned at the moment to point out that if it is un-scientific to draw a hard and fast line between the functional and the organic, it would also seem to be opposed to Christian principle to believe that what Christ and his disciples did through faith in God and man, his followers are excluded from doing or trying to do. That there is a vast difference in power is obvious, but it is a difference surely of degree rather than of kind. The words of the Master himself could be quoted in support of this: but let us look at facts as they present themselves to any unprejudiced observer.

Spiritual healing has, or should have, as its primary object the healing of the human spirit through contact with the Divine Spirit; the healing of the body is included, for health in the right sense of the word is wholeness, i.e. health of spirit, soul and body. Jesus was a healer; to life he was concerned to bring more life in all its aspects and fullness. But while the healing of the body was to him of much importance, it is clear that he did not put this in the first place. 'Fear not them which destroy the body, but fear him that can destroy both soul and body in hell.' The health of the whole personality was to him of first importance and had to be preserved at all costs. 'If your right hand offend you, cut it off.' That no doubt has its application to the moral life, but also to the physical. A gangrenous limb must be amputated if the health of the organism is at stake. This should help us to accept the fact that sooner or later the body must deteriorate and die. Death itself can be accepted as a cutting off of the whole body to liberate the spirit, so that the person may have a freer and fuller life.

If health of soul is the primary object of spiritual healing it follows that we should not expect its effects upon the body to be necessarily immediate. True, something of supreme importance takes place immediately, but the full result and benefit of this happening may not be immediately secured. Now is the time when the patient must exercise all his faith, believing that something has happened, and that, like the grain quickened in the soil by the touch of the sun, bringing forth first the blade, then the ear, and after that the full corn in the ear, it will in due season bear good fruit. Should however the patient think, because he does not see at once all that he looked for, that nothing has happened, and if his doctor supports that conclusion, much harm can be done not only to the body but also to the soul; his faith is weakened and a great opportunity is lost. Wonderful things do happen: in very truth all life is miraculous, but we should expect healing, like any other manifestation of good life, to take a natural course when it has to exert its influence upon a body subject to natural laws. What we may rightly expect is a transformation in the character of their operation. We have to work out this healing, this salvation, not only in fear and trembling, but with great confidence and expectation, for it is God that works in us both to will and to do His good pleasure. He does not seem to be in the hurry that we often are; His mills grind slowly, but they grind exceeding fine. He is eternal as well as temporal, and when we come into a real personal relationship with Him, there is something of these two elements in us also, the temporal and the eternal.

Granting that the primary intention of spiritual healing is health of soul and spirit, another question of much importance emerges. Who is the best judge of this healing? Is it the doctor who examines cases of what he calls paranormal or unorthodox healing from a purely medical and scientific point of view? Or is it the patient who has in mind his whole life rather than his physiology? Sigaud, we remember, defined health very well, I think, as the functional unity of the organism; the organism and the personality unified, integrated for the work it has to do, and for the life it should be living. I venture to think that, if he is right in this, the patient, rather than the doctor, is the better judge of whether he is cured, or not. It depends obviously upon what constitutes a cure.

A patient told me he always felt better when he was not too well, which rather startled me, but it was quite a reasonable remark. He was unhappy, had no confidence in himself, was always apprehensive, feeling that something was wrong. Under these circumstances, an influenza cold, or a pain in his stomach, was a positive relief. Concentrating on this he could forget himself, and felt genuinely better in consequence.

Another patient told me that, following a grave fault on his part, he had been through hell for the last three years. He could neither sleep nor think; he could not feel rightly about things, and had to give up his career. In the end he turned to God, seeking help and guidance. From that moment he began to recover, and is now almost fit to resume his business. This has made such an impression upon him, has so changed his whole attitude to life, that he feels, so he informed me, that what he has been through has been worthwhile; that he would not have missed it.

These cases contrast with the typical neuroses where there may be nothing organically the matter, and yet the patient feels frightful, going from one doctor to another, looking for a cure. Which case, we may well ask, is the more serious of the two? The man with the physical complaint yet feeling well in himself, or the other who without any physical complaint, feels himself to be seriously disordered, needing to be healed?

Health of body is certainly very important: it is what the patient usually comes for, but it should not be the primary concern in spiritual healing; if it is, we cannot object to the doctor considering the case from a purely scientific point of view. If, on the other hand, healing of spirit is the primary matter, then this must be spiritually, not scientifically, discerned.

But faith and reason, religion and science, should go together. Some time ago I saw at Dunsfold in Surrey a healing well, close by the village church. The well had been consecrated, and for centuries had attracted many who suffered from diseases of the eyes. I was told by the vicar that an ophthalmic surgeon from Harley Street, interested in the well, had had the water analysed and had discovered in it some free ammonia and other constituents which, he said, would prove of benefit in certain ophthalmic cases. Today of course we go to a chemist with a prescription; much better no doubt, more hygienic, more scientific, but I wonder whether something has not been lost in the process — and that rather important. For surely the belief that the virtue of the well came from a Divine source had for the pilgrim patients a value that went far beyond the merely physical. The water to them was holy water; the place whereon they stood was holy ground.

And the question I found myself asking was this. Need

the discovery of some chemical property in the water necessarily destroy the faith which gave the whole situation its real power? As we grow more scientific, need we grow less devout? If it is better to go to the ophthalmic surgeon and the chemist for the lotion he prescribes, need we lose the faith which doubles or quadruples the value of their service?

It would indeed be sad if in any good we lost a greater good. Is it unreasonable to believe that a physician who acknowledges the Divine character of all healing and the spiritual nature with which he is himself endowed, can support the faith of his patient and supply what science in itself must lack? This surely is what religion and science working together should achieve, fulfilling the prophecy of our Lord that even greater works than He did we should do.

Through his relationship with the patient, and by his skill and knowledge, the physician may open up a way along which the Divine Healer may come. In this he will surely welcome the support of relatives and friends through their prayers, and the means of grace provided by the Christian Church in its worship and sacraments. In the sympathetic attitude provided by this support, the conditions under which healing can take place are much more favourable than in homes where there is no such faith, and where spiritual means are discounted.

I hope I have said enough to make clear the fact that spiritual healing is not to be regarded as an alternative to other means of healing, nor even as supplementary to them; rather it should inspire all the means, physical and mental, which God puts at our disposal. It is not a new form of therapeutics to be tried when other means have failed. Too often it is reserved until the patient is *in extremis* when he may be incapable of full co-operation. I have written elsewhere that it is the sacramental principle for which we contend when I say that spiritual healing should not be restricted in its meaning and application to a few methods such as Unction and the Laying-on of Hands, which may have a very valuable, but necessarily restricted, use and that it should not leave unconsecrated, outside the pale of the spirit, the more usual means provided by science and experience.

I am hopeful that we shall come to see more clearly that spiritual healing is not so much a matter of the means or of the method, as of the motive underlying the method, and of the end to be attained, the establishment of a relationship with God, in which the whole man, body, mind and spirit is in harmony with the Divine Will and Love.

I would stress also the fact that healing springs from something central in the nature of the person. The seed grows from its nucleus, the plant from its root; and these must be sound. So it is in man. 'There is that in us,' writes Dr W. R. Matthews, Dean of St Paul's, 'which is deeper than the experience of our senses, deeper than the intellect, the core and centre of our personality. It is so much ourselves that we can never know it as we can know our mental capacities or our moral character, because it is itself the knower — the subject which can never be object — but it is the point where we are in contact with the Divine Spirit. It is there that 'the Spirit himself beareth witness with our spirit, that we are children of God.' It is there that the healing and sustaining powers of the Divine Spirit operate, unifying and giving vitality to all our human powers; and it is from this centre also that we go out to fulfil in our lives the Divine purpose.

Disease in the last analysis usually denotes a lack of vital power. This can only be made good through contact with the sources of power, and through the use we make of the power which we then possess. Disease always develops and spreads from some focal point; so does health. Here at this centre of personality we take in, and from it we must live out. The realization of this possibility is what we mean by religious faith. Faith, at a certain level, is our belief in a possibility supported by reason and experience: at a higher level it is a matter of personal trust, and that, as Archbishop Temple once said, is vital for the individual. The way into the kingdom of Science is, as Newton said, the same as that into the Kingdom of God — the way of a little child. We must be more conscious of God the Father than of ourselves, of his power than of our weakness, of his healing than of our disease.

In all healing there is a human part and a divine part. As a doctor I have stressed the importance of the former, of realizing what we must do to help ourselves. Too many patients suppose that their part is purely passive. They go from one physician to another looking for the right doctor or the right remedy, when all the time the secret of the cure is in themselves. There is in the nature of man a creative healing power too rarely realized and used. Doctors have something to learn in this respect from certain healers who, believing they possess the gift of healing, use it with confidence. Physicians are too apt to put their entire confidence in medicines and appliances of one sort or another which are only the tools of their trade, leaving themselves out of it. The means at our disposal, whether they be physical or mental, are important but the personal factor, which is also the spiritual, is all-important if

we are treating, not a disease, but a person suffering
from one. Confidence is essential in the relationship of
the patient and his doctor. A psychiatrist employing
suggestion knows that the condition of its success is the
state of receptivity or susceptibility induced in the mind
of the patient. Every specialist knows that the recom-
mendation of the patient's own trusted doctor contri-
butes greatly to the success of his special advice or
skill. The clergyman engaged in the ministry of spiritual
healing values no less the support of the doctor attending
the case.

We should recognise, however, that faith is not itself
the cause of the cure but only the condition of it. Faith
is not the reality we seek but a pathway to it, a pathway
often obstructed by fear or tension, unbelief, or a
consciousness of sin and guilt. As long as this remains,
healing is prevented. The current cannot flow. As a rule
it is not enough to know that there is an obstruction;
one must know what it is, and how it got there before it
can be removed. That is where the skill of the physician
or the psychiatrist comes in.

We do not hear much today about sin. The modern
man, we are told, is not troubling about his sins. But we
hear much about the sense of inferiority, about complexes, anxiety states, fears and obsessions, many of
which the conscious mind may recognise as very
irrational and yet be quite unable to overcome. The
mind can, as a rule, control the body; it can direct
some of its own activities; but can it change itself?
Modern psychology does not believe in the total
depravity of human nature but its teaching certainly
supports the dictum of Jeremiah that the heart may be
deceitful above all things and desperately wicked. Out
of it, as our Lord said, come many great evils, but it is

no less true that from it comes also the best of which we are capable. In view of these facts there is good reason to think that the practice of confession is good both for the soul and the body. The therapeutic value of this with the absolution which follows is immeasurable.

Professor J. S. Stewart in his Lyman Beecher Lectures at Yale University said, 'We are hearing much in these days about the Church and the ministry of healing. We are being told — I for one believe quite truly — that the Church has too much neglected this part of its commission. But I submit that in this whole debate there is one fact that is too often overlooked. It is this — *that wherever the Church truly proclaims the forgiveness of sins there the healing ministry is veritably at work*. Who can tell the incalculable results of the word of absolution for the integration of human personalities? Who can say how many demons are being exorcized, how many potentialities of mental trouble, neurasthenia and even organic diseases are being rooted out by the assurance of pardon and renewal? 'I always send my patients,' said a distinguished psychiatrist, 'to hear Dr So-and-so preach: he preaches the forgiveness of sins.' 'The forgiveness of God, in my opinion,' writes Dr Leslie Weatherhead, 'is the most powerful therapeutic idea in the world.'[1]

Healing has always been associated with cleansing. Instinctively we feel that this must be so. Jesus said to Peter, 'If I wash thee not, thou hast no part with me'. Man cannot meet God, who is Holy, in the sanctuary of his own being unless he is made fit to do so. He needs a saviour as well as a healer. This is why the preaching

[1] *A Faith to Proclaim* by J.S. Stewart (London: Hodder & Stoughton; New York: Charles Scribner's Sons); chap. 2, Proclaiming Forgiveness.

of the gospel and the healing of the sick should go together. They are both rquired. Sometimes the usual sequence is reversed. The patient must become whole in himself before he can be healed in any part of his body. The paralytic man lowered through the roof into the presence of our Lord was first forgiven, his healing followed.

Ten lepers were healed, but to one only was the word said 'Arise, go thy way: thy faith hath made thee whole.' It was to the man who realized the significance of what had happened: that God had come into his life and that this experience would always be his. From that moment he was a different man. All healing is divine. It comes to the body in a way appropriate to it, as it comes to the mind; but to the spirit and soul of man God comes Himself, and only in that relationship is man made whole in the full sense of the word. When this is attained there can be no such thing as failure. The patient may not get all that he expected or desired, that is another matter. Christ endured the cross for the joy that was set before Him. He saw beyond it.

When spiritual healing is effective a new situation has been created, for the patient is in a real sense a different man; he is less anxious or afraid, his tensions have gone. He has that placidity of mind in which alone, as Walter Pater said, the business of the spirit can be done. As a result, treatment which previously was unavailing may now become effective. I have already pointed out the mistake of supposing that all the efforts of the patient and the doctor have been useless because they have not succeeded. They may have been essential for the success of other means. It is no less important that the patient, after receiving spiritual help, should believe that medical, surgical and other measures have now a much greater opportunity of becoming curative. This does not mean that the one should wait for the other, they should go together.

More than this, the patient may himself become a source of healing. Every believer in the healing power and love of God, certainly everyone who has experience of this, is himself potentially a healer. When combined with medical knowledge and skill the possibilities are very great. But many are called to exercise the Ministry of Healing in some measure or way. Most doctors can tell of certain sick rooms from which they never come away without feeling that they themselves have been refreshed and healed: when one man believes another catches the flame.

'Heaven doth with us as we with torches do,
 Not light them for ourselves; for if our virtues
 Did not go forth of us 't were all alike
 As if we had them not. Spirits are not finely touch'd
 But to fine issues.'

APPENDIX ONE

ORGANISATIONS FOR THE PROMOTION OF SPIRITUAL HEALING

The following list includes some of the better known organisations in this country formed to encourage an interest in Divine Healing.

The Churches' Council of Healing, 10 Eaton Gate, London, SW1. For particulars of this Council see p. 3 of the text.

The Guild of Health 'stands for Healing in the widest sense of the word'. It was founded in 1905 and anyone is eligible to join who is 'a member of the Christian Church'. There is no denominational discrimination. One of its declared objects is to 'bring together Christian people, including doctors, psychologists and ministers of religion, to work in fellowship for fuller health both for the individual and the community'. It issues a monthly magazine, *For Health and Healing*, and its headquarters are The Edward Wilson Memorial House, 26 Queen Anne St, W1. Among its patrons and officers are clergy and doctors of high standing in their profession.

The London Healing Mission, 20 Dawson Place, W2, among other aims, sets out under the direction of an Anglican clergyman to 'teach and minister Christ's healing wherever opportunity allows', and to 'co-operate with other Christian healing movements for the advancement of Christ's healing'. A printed letter is sent four times a year to all in fellowship with the Mission. The mission work was carried on at the same house for many years by the Rev. John Maillard who subsequently acted as warden of a home of healing at Milton Abbey, Dorset.

The Healing Life Mission was started more recently by Mr Maillard at Okehampton, Devon, whence he issues a monthly journal under the title *The Healing Life*. He still retains his association with the London Mission as a trustee.

The Divine Healing Mission is also located at Dawson Place. Its monthly magazine, *The Healer*, was started in 1908 by James Moore Hickson, the memory of whose ministry subsequently led to the formation of the Mission. Reference to him is made on pp. 5, 111 of this book. The message proclaimed is 'that our Lord Jesus Christ is the Healer of man's whole being — his body, soul and spirit; and that He came to bring redemption to every creature and to all life hurt or wounded by the transgression of man'. Hickson was one of a notable group of men and women who started the Society of Emmanuel to revive the ministry of healing in the Church. It was dissolved in 1921 after an existence of sixteen years, as it was then considered that its work had been accomplished.

The Guild of St Raphael, unlike the Churches' Council of Healing and the Guild of Health is under purely Anglican patronage and control. Otherwise its main purpose is the same. It came into being in the early years of the First World War.

The Methodist Society for Medical and Pastoral Practice seeks to bring together 'all interested in the religious approach to the problems of healing', in particular doctors, ministers and psychologists, and to serve as a clearing-house of ideas formulated by any such groups that might be set up to study the problems of spiritual healing. This Society owes much to the initiative of Dr Leslie D. Weatherhead, a well-known exponent of the subject.

The Friends Spiritual Healing Fellowship links together members of the Religious Society of Friends and others who are interested in divine healing. A quarterly 'News Letter' is circulated to members and a well patronized rest home has recently been opened at Claridge House, near Lingfield, Surrey.

The Order of St Luke is an International Order, with no denominational barriers, founded by an American Episcopalian priest, himself a healer and an evangelist. The only basis for membership is 'a dedicated discipleship to Jesus Christ, with an awareness of His calling to care for the sick.'

Much might be said also of individual work producing noteworthy results in this field by those who appear to have the gift of healing in more than normal measure. Four examples must suffice for lack of space.

Mr Harry Edwards is well-known as one who not only practises healing but who also writes on the subject. He conducts clinics, which are visited by large numbers of people suffering from a variety of ailments, at The Sanctuary, Shere, Guildford, Surrey and publishes a monthly journal, *The Spiritual Healer*.

Miss Dorothy Kerin has a house at Groombridge, Kent, where patients who need rest and refreshment of spirit rather than medical attention are received. She herself was miraculously cured in 1912 when suffering from the gravest symptoms of tubercular meningitis and other complications, being pronounced by her doctors in a hopeless condition. She has told the story in a little book called *The Living Touch*, published by Justin Powys. Since this remarkable experience Miss Kerin has spent her life in ministering to others.

Her book chanced to be the first to fall into my hands on spiritual healing and I read it with greater attention than I might otherwise have done because, in the Preface, an old Cambridge tutor of mine, Dr G. F. C. Searle, F.R.S., was quoted as warmly commending it. I knew him well and had a high regard for him. He himself had come to have a strong belief in spiritual healing and his virile personality was a striking testimony to this belief. He died very recently in his ninetieth year.

Brother Mandus, as he is called since he became a prominent figure in the spiritual healing world, has a sanctuary at 476, Lytham Road, Blackpool. He frequently holds meetings for healing purposes in London and other parts of the country, and his addresses and ministerings seem to be widely appreciated. He has started a World Healing Crusade and the activities of this and other kindred movements are recorded in a monthly journal, *The Crusader*. The services of healers like Harry Edwards and Brother Mandus are given freely to all who seek them.

Mr Godfrey Mowatt was consecrated by Archbishop Temple as a minister of divine healing and he has been engaged in this personal service for many years, in close association with The Churches' Council of Healing.

I have selected these four from among several others whom I might have mentioned because I can write of them from first-hand knowledge.

APPENDIX TWO

NOTE ON THE CURES AT LOURDES

The following particulars were kindly supplied to me by a doctor who accompanies invalids on their pilgrimage to Lourdes.

'Before an invalid goes to Lourdes on a pilgrimage the Medical Officer of the pilgrimage has a certificate of the invalid's condition in his possession. This certificate is furnished by the patient's own doctor. If that invalid is suddenly cured at Lourdes, he or she is taken to the Medical Bureau there and examined by a panel of doctors consisting of the Head resident doctor and as many doctors as possible of the other pilgrimages. Sometimes there are as many as one hundred doctors of all nationalities present.

'If the case is worth recording a dossier is prepared by the Head of the Bureau and statements are taken first of all from the invalid of the "happening" and, secondly, signed statements of the findings of a few of the doctors present who had examined the invalid. In appropriate cases X-ray photograph-cardiographs are taken on the spot. The dossier is kept at Lourdes and the invalid is told to return in a year's time.

'When the pilgrimage arrives home the Medical Officer of the pilgrimage gets in touch with the invalid's own doctor and he is asked to furnish a statement of his examination and present condition of the invalid, together with specialist reports, X-ray findings, etc., both before and after the cure. These are all sent to Lourdes to build up the dossier and to await next year's examination. Should a miraculous happening be recorded at this meeting, the miraculee is asked to attend a meeting of the Medical Society of Our Lady of Lourdes, which is held annually in Paris in order to confirm cases. So really there is not much chance of a loophole.

'Whilst I was in Lourdes this year I saw the dossier of a French boy, whose case was accepted as a first-class miracle by the doctors. It appears that on coming to Lourdes this year he had been completely blind as a result of an infectious disease which occurred when he was four years old. He was now eleven, and whilst making "the stations of the Cross" he suddenly bent down and picked up a twig showing it to his mother. On being examined at the Bureau by the doctors it was found that he could see quite well with both eyes, although from a medical point of view he was still blind, both optic nerves being apparently useless and pathologically dead. His field of vision was restricted at first but was soon afterwards extended to normal. Twelve months later he remained in the same condition, seeing perfectly, whilst the optic nerves appeared to be still dead. The following year, however, the nerves took on their normal function and appearance and his sight was perfect in both eyes.

'As an example of a case that was not accepted, we had an invalid who was semi-paralysed for seven years from the waist down, as a result of a fractured vertebra. He had been hit by a travelling crane. During the procession of the sick at Lourdes he suddenly regained the full use of his limbs. On investigation it was found that one specialist had said in his notes — previous to his going to Lourdes — that there was an element of hysteria in his case. That was sufficient for it to be turned down.'

The following additional information was sent by another doctor, one of the officers of the Council of the Guild of St Luke, SS Cosmas and Damian. In considering the case history of any patient alleged to have been cured at Lourdes, the panel of doctors examining the evidence take into full account the quality and professional status of the patient's medical advisers. The intention is to prove beyond all reasonable doubt that 'no clinical explanation of the cure can be advanced and that it is evidently beyond reach of the laws of nature'. The last words must be taken to mean, presumably, the laws of nature in so far as man has hitherto been able to fathom them.

The above statements possibly go some way to explain the conclusion reached by Dr Leslie Weatherhead in his *Psychology, Religion and Healing*, that at least ninety-eight per cent. of the sick who visit Lourdes return uncured. The remaining two per cent. may well be the very small proportion of cases officially accepted as cured after the most careful medical scrutiny described in these letters.